HEARING
VOICES

HEARING VOICES

Creating, Voicing and Producing Great Radio Commercials

by
Alan Barzman
Somewhat autobiographical,
fairly instructional
& slightly critical

Gabriel Publications

Published by:
Gabriel Publications
14340 Addison St. #101
Sherman Oaks, California 91423
(818) 906-2147 Voice
(818) 990-8631 Fax
www.GabrielBooks.com

HEARING VOICES by Barzman & Company (dba BarzRadio)
Copyright © 2003 Alan Barzman
All rights reserved.
ISBN # 1-891689-83-5
Library of Congress Catalog Card Number: 2002102502

Distributed by: Partners Book Distributors
Editors: Renée Ergazos and Rennie Gabriel
Typography: Synergistic Data Systems, sdsdesign@altrionet.com
Cover Design: Dale Schroeder, SDS

Manufactured in the United States of America.

Table of Contents

About the Author. 7

Preface 8

1. Hear Comes the Parade 11

2. Return with Us Now to Those Thrilling
   Days of Yesteryear 15

3. Radio: A Little Dab Won't Do Ya 25

4. Why Can't a Radio Commercial
   Work like a Newspaper Ad? 33

5. Yours Truly, the Creative Genius 39

6. Once Outside the Pit. 49

7. Capturing the Listener: A Secret Is Revealed . . . 53

8. A Radio Commercial: Writing
   It and Presenting It. 59

9. Humor 67

10. Who's on First? 81

11. When Looking for a Forest Can
    Mean Missing a Tree 93

12. When You've Just Made the
    World's Funniest Radio Commercial. 99

13. Clang, Bam, Crash, Boing,
    Clunk and Silence. 107

14. Music and Jingles:
    The Artificial Sweeteners. 115

15. Producing Radio Commercials:
    First We'll Need Some Voices 119

16. Doing Voice Work:
    To Aspire or Not to Aspire. 125

17. The Recording Studio:
    The Commercial's Moment of Truth 139

18. The Phantom Recording Session:
    Where Is Everybody? 145

19. The Last Act:
    Finishing the Radio Commercial 147

20. Thanks for Listening 155

    Bibliography 157

About the Author

ALAN BARZMAN, (BarzRadio) has devoted his career in advertising exclusively to the making of humorous radio commercials.

He is a recipient of the Radio Advertising Bureau's Orson Welles Award for Creative Excellence, as well as receiving the Clio Awards, International Broadcast Awards, London Advertising Awards, ADDY and ANDY Awards and many others.

Advertisers who have availed themselves of Mr. Barzman's creative radio production services include American Express, McDonalds, *People Magazine*, Delta Airlines, Kemper Insurance, Paine Webber, KFC, Pepsi Cola, Ford Electronics, Anheuser Busch and GTE. Some of this work was done when he was partnered with Bert Berdis in the acclaimed radio production firm Bert & Barz & Company.

In addition to his creative and producing skills, Mr. Barzman is also a well known voice talent. His highly recognizable and familiar voice has been heard on countless radio and television commercials. Most notably he was the original voice-over who prompted the Energizer Bunny to keep "going and going and going."

Mr. Barzman is a graduate of the University of Oregon and received a Master's degree in Communications from Boston University.

BarzRadio
barz@barzradio.com

Preface

When it comes to the making of radio advertising or any advertising, coming up with "the big idea" is a lot like spotting one of those comets that cross the skies once every ninety years. It's a fairly rare occurrence.

Small ideas, on the other hand, are much like shooting stars. If you look closely enough, one or more might come darting across the creative heavens every other night. Of course, small ideas are most acceptable in this business, but it's the big ones that are stratospheric!

One day I got a phone call at my office. It was from an executive/creative/broadcast director/producer-person whom I kind of knew at an advertising agency here in Los Angeles. I detected a tone of urgency in his voice as he asked me if I could drop everything and come right over and have a little meeting with him. An hour later, I am there. "Little" my foot, this turned out to be big, just like the idea he would be asking me to come up with.

"We have this large national account," he begins to explain, as if he really needed to. Who didn't know that they had this large national account, and who also didn't know that it was their only account?

"Well next year," he went on, "this client has decided to put their entire advertising budget into radio."

"Wow."

"We're planning to spend so much money in radio, it looks like we're going to need to do about a hundred different commercials, maybe even more."

"Whoa."

"We were thinking that we'd like to hire you and your company to write and produce all of them.

"Hold me."

"Here's the thing," he said, as I felt myself slipping into a mild catatonic stupor, "we don't want you to start doing anything just yet, I mean, not until after our meeting next Tuesday with the client."

"Tuesday. . . meeting. . . client."

"Yeah, that's when we're going to sew everything up. You know, cross all the *T*s, dot all the *I*s."

"Dot tees. . . cross eyes."

"Right. Now it would really be great if we could go into this meeting and knock 'em dead. I mean, totally blow the client away."

"Kill. . . client."

"Right, you know, with a big idea. But really, we don't want you to start writing anything. Just give it a little thought. Maybe after you go home, something might come to you in the shower."

"Go home. . . take shower."

"Don't even put anything down on paper. Just call and tell me the idea and I'll go in and present it. I know it'll be great."

"Present. . . great. . . idea."

"You got it. The bigger the better. But honestly, only if something comes to you. By tomorrow would be perfect."

Well, by tomorrow, which was the next morning, I phoned him.

You see, the day before, which would have been yesterday, after I had met with him, I immediately went home and took nine showers. Sure enough, half-way through the last one, a big idea came to me.

What this big idea was, is not really that important. When a big idea doesn't end up ending up, there's not much reason to keep it hanging around in your brain. Unless you're planning to save the idea with the hopes of trying to unload it on some other advertiser down the road, which never seems to work out anyhow. In which case, one just tends to let the idea slip away, which is what I did. So don't ask me what the idea was, because I really don't remember. But I can assure you, it was a big and especially terrific idea for radio.

When I phoned him with the idea, he could hardly contain his joy and said that he'd call me at my office the very minute the meeting with their client was over, which he did.

"Barz," he said, in a somber tone of voice, which forebodingly spoke of a less than successful meeting, "it looks like I've got some good news and some bad news."

"Oookay," I said, bracing myself for the worst while wanting to save the best for last, "so, what's the bad news?"

"Well, since we spoke last week, the client has had a complete change of mind. Now they don't want to do any radio."

Suddenly I felt a stupor coming on again. "Client. . . changed mind. . . now. . . no radio."

"Right, no radio. But Barz, for what it's worth, let me tell you the good news."

"Good news. . . yes. . . tell Barz good news."

"The client really loved your idea."

Know what I did? I went home and took another shower.

Hear Comes the Parade

Radio, unceremoniously became official on November 2, 1920, when station KDKA in Pittsburgh aired the first sanctioned broadcast. This historic event was the airing of the Harding/Cox presidential election returns.

Even though the audience receiving this broadcast only consisted of a smattering of audiophiles, it did herald a very special era that lasted until the end of the 1940s. This era is fondly and nostalgically called "The Golden Age of Radio."

Along with what soon became a seemingly endless parade of entertaining programs and shows, as well as news, sports and special events coverage, radio listeners eventually began to hear a proliferation of something else in the broadcasting mix. It was advertising—specifically, radio commercials. While these little "ads of the airwaves" quickly became synonymous with the programs and shows they were sponsoring, no one seems sentimentally inclined to call this same era "The Golden Age of Radio Commercials."

Today's sound of radio bears little semblance to what radio sounded like then. The same, however, cannot be said of radio commercials. While the sound of radio may have dramatically changed over the years, the sound of radio commercials has remained fairly static.

Radio programmers know that in order to attract and keep listeners, their programming must be compelling. They must innovate and be creative. Conversely, many advertisers seldom attend to this important consideration and should know that listeners seldom choose or even want to listen to radio commercials. The reason is that there is little, if anything, in the content of radio commercials that's compelling enough to make them care to listen.

Mistakenly, too many advertisers today subscribe to the belief that pure product copy, or sales event information alone, is compelling reason enough to listen. This information is, of course, compelling to the advertiser, but seldom to the radio listener.

Although commercials may certainly be heard, it is my contention that few are really listened to. In the early days of radio, this was not necessarily the case. People enjoyed commercials, therefore, they listened. Commercials weren't perceived as interruptions but were regarded as being informative and helpful when making product purchasing decisions.

Another factor contributing to the acceptance of radio commercials was that the products they were advertising were closely associated with the popularity of the stars and programs they were sponsoring. When it came to gaining a share of market, those products consistently being advertised on radio's most popular programs were the benefactors of the lion's share.

Radio was the call to listen to programs like *Jack Benny, Burns & Allen, Lum 'n Abner, I Love a Mystery, The Shadow* and *Pepper Young's Family.*

The commercials were the call to buy products like Jello, Johnsons Wax, Life Buoy Soap, Wheaties, Ovaltine, Barbasol, Texaco and Maxwell House Coffee. However, no one sounded the call louder and clearer than Johnnie, the little Philip Morris bellhop, when he stood up at the microphone and called out "Call For Phil-lip Morr-eess."

By sponsoring radio shows, advertisers or "sponsors" as they were called, soon became identified with these shows as well as becoming identified with the show's stars. "This is Bob 'Pepsodent' Hope" and Jack Benny's famous "Jello-Again."

More often than not, a sponsor's name was even wrangled into the name of the show: The Kraft Music Hall with Bing Crosby, The Pabst Blue Ribbon Show with Eddie Cantor, The Chase and Sanborn Hour with Edgar Bergan & Charlie McCarthy, and The Lux Radio Theater.

For the advertisers, things couldn't have been better. People liked the shows, ergo they liked the sponsors, ergo they liked the sponsors' products, ergo they even liked the sponsors' commercials.

A few years into this era, in a Midwestern cornfield, a compelling call of a different kind was being heard. It was the call of farmer Fred Petzel calling his hogs. You know, "sooey-sooey?" This was no ordinary "sooey-sooey." It was a world class call that eventually made Fred Petzel the National Hog Calling Champion.

You may be thinking, "What does this have to do with radio advertising?"

Moments after Fred Petzel won this coveted award, a radio reporter stuck a microphone in front of his face and said, "Tell our listening audience, to what do you attribute your hog calling prowess?" Whereupon Fred drawled, "Why that's easy. The power and the appeal must be in the voice. You gotta let them hogs know you got something for 'em."

See the connection? Although Fred Petzel's unique expertise lay in a totally unrelated field, a man with those motivational skills and that way with words certainly makes him, in my book, radio advertising's very first pundit.

Chapter 2

Return with Us Now to Those Thrilling Days of Yesteryear

In the first two decades of the twentieth century, the advertisers' medium of choice was print. Of course, print was the advertisers' only choice. Advertisers were comfortable with print. Whether it was newspaper, magazines, catalogs, pamphlets, posters, flyers or even sandwich boards, the medium of print suited them just fine. Why not? Print did a good job for them. What else could an advertiser possibly want or need? Well, "what else" was lurking just around the corner. It was, what else, radio.

When radio first hit the airwaves, it was seen as little more than a ho-hum event. The Harding/Cox Presidential Election Returns didn't exactly portend of better listening pleasures to come.

For those behind radio broadcasting, nobody's corporate light bulb initially snapped on with a business plan envisioning vast revenues from selling air time to advertisers. Most, including radio pioneer, Westinghouse, saw a modest monetary future in the sales of inexpensive radio sets. (Today many of those early sets are worth their weight in bakelite on the old-radios collector's market.)

If one is going to produce and market radio sets, shouldn't there be a good reason for people to buy one or two? That good reason was, of course, entertaining programming.

Before you could say, "faster than a speeding bullet," radio was awash in a tidal wave of programs and shows. There was everything from *Superman* to *I Love A Mystery* to *The World Series* to *Fibber McGee & Molly,* and *Easy Aces* in between. Best of all, radio was free—no cost, no obligation. You didn't even have to leave home to enjoy it.

Of course, for radio to continue offering so much for nothing, something had to come along to make it turn a profit. That something, turned out to be advertising, but advertising didn't exactly come along right on the heels of Harding & Cox. Actually, it was a little slow in coming, because there was considerable opposition. Many, including prominent politicians and lawmakers, were not keen on the idea that advertisers would be hawking their laundry detergents and toothpastes over the public airwaves, beaming their "seamy" messages into the privacy and sanctity of peoples' homes. Even the respected advertising trade publication, *Printers Ink* said, "We are opposed to radio advertising for the same reason we are opposed to sky writing. People should not be forced to read or hear advertising, unless they are so inclined." Apparently *Printers Ink* didn't mind outdoor advertising and all the Burma Shave signs that were starting to crop up along our nation's roadways. However, opposition eventually waned and by the mid 1920s, radio advertising, seamy and otherwise, was wending its way into the privacy and sanctity of peoples' homes.

Once advertisers were given the green light, many weren't ready to make the leap. They were not convinced that radio was a viable advertising medium. The idea of going from the comfort of print into the uncertainty of radio didn't make much sense. "In print," these radio skeptics reasoned, you can see a photograph or illustration of the product. You can see the name of the product and you can make the product or the product's name as big as you want. You can even see a picture of people consuming or using the product." "In radio," they argued, who's going to buy something that they can't see?" That concern, of course, was quickly dispelled.

One memorable example from the annals of radio lore has it that Louella Parsons, the legendary Hollywood gossip columnist, sponsored by Campbell's Soup, got a little carried away one night on her radio program. It seems that Ms. Parsons suddenly began to extemporaneously wax eloquent about her favorite Campbell's soup: Cream of Tomato.

As the story goes, thanks to her spontaneous testimonial on the radio, the demand at the markets for Campbell's Cream of Tomato was so overwhelming, that back at the Campbell's plant they quickly ran out of that soup. Case closed. Advertising on radio can get people to buy a product even if they can't see it.

Maybe our friend Fred Petzel, the hog calling champ, did hit his head on the nail when he said, "The power and the appeal must be in the voice."

Today, many advertisers pay handsomely for celebrities and famous sports figures to appear or be heard in their commercials. It's called "a celebrity endorsement." Advertisers have learned that the power and appeal of the voice, or at least the voice's persona, is perhaps, just as important as the selling message.

Celebrity voices not withstanding, a typical radio commercial of that era would usually feature the friendly and dulcet tones of a rich, baritone voice. It was the voice of "The Announcer." It was the announcer's smooth and confident style of delivery that conveyed a sense of assurance and trust. The announcer was truly the soul of the commercial. Thanks to him, radio listeners were inclined to believe just about anything that the radio commercial told them to believe.

In those early days, many actors found that their performing destiny lay not necessarily on the stage soliloquizing in *Hamlet* but usually in front of a microphone soliloquizing in radio commercials. Hence the term *commercial actor.*

The backbone of the product sell, however, was "The Jingle." It was the late David Ogilvy, one of advertising's best known pundits, who once suggested "When there isn't much to say in your advertising, sing it." Well, lots of advertisers did just that. In media terms, "lots" refers to frequency and in terms of radio advertising's ultimate effectiveness, frequency is an essential way to help insure that effectiveness.

A commercial with music and singing was called a jingle. Where the term *jingle* comes from, nobody seems to know. My guess is that it has something to do with Santa Claus, but I'm not sure why.

Musically, jingles could best be described as simple and trite. Yet it was the consistent familiarity of these banal, little ditties that still bang around in peoples' heads. At least in the heads of those who remember: "Have you tried Wheaties?/ The best breakfast food in the Land"/ "Pepsi-Cola hits the spot/Twelve full ounces that's a lot/Twice as much for a nickel too/Pepsi Cola is the drink for you."/ "Poor Miriam/Poor Miriam/ Neglected using Irium/Sweet Miriam/Sweet Miriam/Now she's using Irium."

You may be wondering, "What the heck is Irium?" Back then, nobody seemed to wonder. If they heard it on the radio, that was good enough for them. People believed what the commercials told them and Pepsodent told listeners that Irium was a "mystery teeth whitening ingredient," found only in their toothpaste. What Pepsodent neglected to tell listeners, was that Irium was also a "fictitious" teeth whitening ingredient. There was no such thing as Irium. It was merely a figment of a copywriter's imagination. Do you remember Solium? Solium was the special "sunshine ingredient" that made clothes "whiter than white" when washed with Rinso. ("Rinso White/Rinso Bright.")

The only difference between Solium and Irium was that Solium didn't rhyme as well with Mirium. I suppose that if the copywriter who came up with Solium had been working on the Pepsodent account instead of Rinso, then nobody would have heard of poor Miriam. Chances are, Solium would've probably showed up in Pepsodent's commercials, as the special sunshine ingredient that made teeth "whiter than white."

Some of the most visible radio advertisers of that era were the tobacco companies. If one was to believe what Philip Morris had to say, one could conclude that there was even a health benefit with smoking their cigarettes. Here's a blurb of announcer copy from an early radio commercial. "Remember: Top ranking doctors, eminent nose and throat specialists actually suggest Philip Morris in cases of irritation due to smoking. Above all remember this: You'll be glad tomorrow, you smoked Philip Morris today." How prophetic.

So where were the truth-in-advertising police? Well, they didn't seem to be around. Advertisers were at liberty to say just about anything they wanted to say and nobody was there to tell them otherwise.

Legal departments at ad agencies didn't exist as we know them today. Hyperbole reigned and radio listeners got an earful of the stuff that unsubstantiated advertising claims were made of. The curious thing is that no one seemed to mind.

If the announcer was the voice and soul of the commercial and the jingle was the backbone, then the slogan must have been the heart and lungs. "Outstanding. And They Are Mild." "Tide's in-Dirt's Out." "Push Pull, Click Click, Change Blades That Quick." "I'd Walk a Mile for a Camel." "L/S/M/F/T... Lucky Strike Means Fine Tobacco."

If this sounds familiar, it's because it still is familiar. The only difference today, is that someone in advertising might tell you that a slogan is essential in a commercial because it helps brand the product. Of course back then, branding was something that was usually done to the hindquarters of cattle.

If nothing else, a slogan in the context of a radio commercial does make it perfectly clear that what the listener hears is indeed a radio commercial.

For me, the king of slogans was Lucky Strike cigarettes. It seemed that every time you turned on the radio, you'd hear a new one. One that I seemed to hear a lot when I was young was "Be Happy Go Lucky." I remember thinking "Someday when I grow up, I'm going to smoke Lucky Strikes. Then I'll always be happy." Do you suppose they were trying to reach kids with that slogan, or were they just targeting me?

Another of their slogans was, perhaps, the first concerted attempt to target a specific segment of the population. In this instance, it was a very significant segment: women. This slogan was based on Lucky's desire to encourage more of them to smoke cigarettes.

It was their contention that women were the major consumers of candy. Of course, in marketing and advertising circles today, that contention would be called a "hypothesis." Before acting upon the hypothesis or hunch, it would first be subjected to the scientific validation of consumer research, like sampling and focus groups.

One thing that they could easily conclude was that candy had lots of calories and cigarettes didn't have any. So Lucky came up with another slogan, a helpful hint for women to curb their sweet tooth. "Reach for a Lucky Instead of a Sweet." It was implicitly permissible for men to take the hint too, but women were the target.

No sooner had Lucky Strike hit the air with this slogan, then they found themselves potentially up to their cigarette butts in pending litigation. It seems that the slogan didn't sit too well with the folks in the candy industry. Sensing that they were on to something pretty darned good, Lucky was not about to completely scrap this slogan, so they modified it slightly: "Reach For a Lucky Instead." Well, the candy people weren't exactly thrilled, but the modification did manage to mollify the candy lawyers.

Still on the kick to enlist more women, World War II gave Lucky Strike the opportunity to come up with what was perhaps the mother of all their slogans. For the folks on the home front, the war was a time of shortages, gas rationing, air raid drills, war bond drives and copious amounts of patriotism. It was also a time when Lucky Strike decided to do some more modifying, this time to their cigarette package design. It was no more than changing from the familiar green background on their package to the "color" white.

Supposedly, the reason for this color change was that the American Tobacco Company's chairman, George Washington Hill, fictitiously depicted in the movie *The Hucksters*, as the tyrannical client who spat on the conference room table, didn't like the color green. I find it ironic that given Mr. Hill's aversion to the color green, his characterization in *The Hucksters* was portrayed by Sidney Greenstreet.

A population of smokers increasingly peopled with women was emerging as a lucrative market for cigarette makers, so Mr. Hill's aversion to green was further exacerbated by his contention that women didn't like this color. However, according to his intuitive insights, women had no problem with the "color" white.

This was his hypothesis and it was one that nobody in the employ of the American Tobacco Company tested, refuted or challenged. The least of whom, were the marketing people who dutifully proceeded to change the Lucky Strike package from green to white.

Lucky Strike's advertising agency was then brought into the picture to address this new color change. They were given the challenging task of coming up with a slogan that would announce as well as lend some credible reason for Lucky Strike's unexpected new packaging.

The creative people came through with flying colors. What they came up with should rank at the top on The Audacious Advertising Implausible Tie-in Scale: "Lucky Strike Green Has Gone to War."

Was that patriotic or what? Not only was uncle William, cousin Todd and the kid next door all going off to war but so was Lucky Strike's color green. After all, wasn't patriotism all about giving up something and doing without it? In Lucky's case, what they were giving up and doing without was the color green.

For cigarette smokers, lighting up a Lucky became more than just an impulsive way to satisfy a nicotine craving. It was also a way of sending a smoke signal salute of gratitude to Lucky Strike for the patriotic thing they were doing for the war effort. What was that patriotic thing? They were trying to get more women to smoke their cigarettes!

Shortages notwithstanding, I have never been convinced that Lucky Strike's contribution of the color green played much of a role in bringing the axis powers to their knees. On the other hand, it did turn out to be a stroke of strategic brilliance in tobacco advertising's hard fought battle to win the brand loyalty of the American smoker, which was beginning to include many more women.

Did the color green, or lack of it, really have anything to do with either winning the war and/or getting more women to smoke? I think about this a lot.

Chapter 3

Radio: A Little Dab Won't Do Ya

During the Golden Age of Radio, advertisers reaped bountiful rewards from this new medium. They and their advertising agencies learned something that many advertisers today have either forgotten or have never learned. The dividends of radio advertising accrue and compound the more an advertiser consistently stays in the medium. However, these dividends seldom materialize immediately following the initial airing of the advertising.

Unlike a lot of advertisers today, who seem to randomly and tentatively dabble in radio, the early radio advertisers were committed to the medium. They were in it for the long haul. During most of that period, the dangling carrot of television was neither an enticing distraction nor even a remote reality for these advertisers, but radio was where they were. What these advertisers discovered was that when a product's radio commercials continuously make positive, memorable and lasting impressions upon listeners, then sooner or later the vast majority of those listeners will buy that product.

However, today there's a much different advertising mind-set. Advertisers are restless and impatient. Cash flows, inventory control and bottom lines wag the tails of advertising and marketing strategies. These strategies demand immediate results, and if results are not immediate, then the advertising is deemed to be ineffective. "Urgency" is the selling proposition, while the commercial's creative approach is relegated to nothing more than hyping this proposition.

Using radio in this manner, is a knee-jerk reaction to what retail merchants have traditionally come to expect from their newspaper advertising. It's a formula of sorts: "X number of sales the next day, as a result of yesterday's newspaper ad, equals enough profits from sales directly related to the response from the ad to pay for the cost of the ad. Sales over that are profit." The arithmetic gets even better when a store's vendors contribute co-op money to help pay for the cost of the ad. When that same equation is applied to radio though it doesn't always "ad" up.

In yesteryear's radio, most of the advertisers were national consumer brands. About the closest any came to an immediate results-driven commercial was to suggest to young listeners, "Tell Mom to buy our cereal or chocolate drink, then tear off the box top or peel off the label and send in for a Little Orphan Annie decoder badge or a Captain Midnight secret ring." Occasionally they'd add, "Include a quarter," or "hurry, offer ends soon." That was, by and large, the extent of an immediate results driven commercial. Even so, radio advertising during the golden age of radio was responsible for making many of those brand products some of today's household names. It's radio that's credited with being the original "image building" medium and the foundations for building those images were not laid and set in concrete overnight.

In spite of all that advertisers were enjoying from radio, by the mid 1940s, after World War II came to an end, it also looked like radio would too. As much as they had honored, cherished and even loved radio, the advertisers honeymoon with it was just about over. To put it more bluntly, "the marriage was just about over."

Advertisers were now smitten with a seductive, new heart throb: television. Everything people had been accustomed to hearing on radio was about to be seen on television. The idea that advertisers could show, demonstrate and even make their products sing, dance and do somersaults on that little TV screen right in peoples' living rooms, was a marketing dream come true. Conversely, this dream was looming as radio's worst nightmare. Was this curtains for radio? Well almost. But hold on. Wait a minute. Don't touch that dial.

What if radio reinvented itself and did something that television wouldn't be doing? (At least, not until Dick Clark came along with *The American Bandstand*.) That's it, radio would play records—you know, music? And they'd play it all the time. Well, most of the time anyway. Sort of like a jukebox. Actually, "a great, big jukebox." was exactly what this new kind of radio was called.

Meanwhile, on Madison Avenue, they were dancing in the street as a change of another kind was being celebrated. It was the creative bail out from radio to television commercials.

If advertisers were charged up about the prospect of seeing their commercials on television, how excited do you suppose their agencies were about putting them there? "Pictures! Now I get to make pictures." That was the gleeful cry from copywriters everywhere.

By no means was this the end of radio commercials, but when an occasional radio assignment did come along, being asked to write it was tantamount to being sent to Siberia. In fact, most radio writing chores were merely handed down to a junior or neophyte writer. "Here kid, go cut your creative teeth on this." At many agencies today, the more senior creatives still slough off radio that way.

By the early 1950s, broadcasting's new era was in full swing and the golden age of radio was becoming a fading sound wave. TV viewers were now being re-introduced to many old radio favorites like Jack Benny, Bob Hope, Burns and Allen, the Lone Ranger, Arthur Godfrey and Milton Berle, as well as new favorites, like Howdy Doody, Kukla Fran & Ollie, Sid Ceasar, Jackie Gleason and Steve Allen.

As for this new brand of radio, listeners were now tuning-in to disc jockeys, top-forty and other formats of music, as well as news, sports, weather, traffic reports and time and temperature.

People were getting used to a different kind of radio and a whole new way of listening to it. They were listening in the bedroom, bathroom, kitchen, backyard, at the beach, in the work place and, of course, in the car.

Because of the profusion of music, radio was now blending into the background. While people listened, they were also doing other things. Curiously, they were watching television the same way they used to listen to radio: curled up or stretched out in front of it. No need to look into their imaginations for the pictures anymore. Now all that people had to do was peer into that small, black and white screen.

Practically overnight, the medium of radio, which had largely been a consortium of radio stations broadcasting network originated shows and programs, was reemerging as a vast assortment of independent, one market radio-station entities, each with its own format of music and on-air personalities. The competition for a slice, make that "morsel," of the advertisers' pie became intense.

Every radio station had a sales staff, usually consisting of two departments: national sales and local sales. National sales were primarily generated by the various stations' national rep. companies. Revenues from national brand advertisers were never sufficient enough to keep these radio stations in the black, so it was left to their local sales people to generate the needed additional revenues from the local advertisers.

To build a local sales department, radio stations were obliged to hire people with no sales experience in this field. It was not uncommon for someone to abruptly quit a job selling shoes, cars, vacuum cleaners or encyclopedias and then take a job the next day at a radio station selling "air-time."

When it came to a knowledge or even an understanding of what radio could or could not do for an advertiser, the people in radio sales relied more on tenacity than know-how. With dogged determination they would hit the street each day in search of prospective radio advertisers. To make the sale, (they were on commission) they tended to over-sell radio, as if it were some sort of holy grail waiting for the retail merchant to discover. "Reach and grasp" were the buzz words and the one station in the market best at reaching and grasping was, naturally, theirs.

Right from the start, however, radio sales people found that they were facing a tough, up-hill selling struggle, because the retail merchants were happily content to be where they were, advertising in the newspaper.

Today, the legacy more or less continues as print remains the preferred medium for most retailers. Obviously, the retail advertisers who can afford it prefer to be in television.

Any local merchant who had been or was currently advertising in the newspaper, could expect a sales call from any number of radio stations in the market and that usually included all of them.

Because radio had mainly been the exclusive advertising domain of the rich and famous national advertisers, small retailers found that their curiosity was piqued. The notion that they too could now join the fraternity of radio advertisers was curiously compelling. All that was needed was some reasonable convincing.

This convincing issue was collectively addressed by those selling radio by simply slamming the media of print, specifically, newspaper. To the people in radio, newspaper was the enemy; to the retailer, it was their comfort zone, safety net and security blanket all rolled into one.

Radio's selling strategy was a battle plan. Attack newspaper and relentlessly bombard the retail merchants, challenging them to a comparative test.

As if speaking with one voice, radio sales people everywhere were saying essentially the same thing, "Try radio. Take the same money you'd spend to run a newspaper ad and make a radio commercial out of the ad. And then run the ad . . . er the commercial, on our radio station. We could put you on the air tomorrow. How 'bout once in morning and once in afternoon drive times and then twice between ten p.m. and midnight? Talk about reach and grasp, do you realize that more people would hear your commercial on our radio station tomorrow than all of the people who will climb Mt. Everest in the next thousand years? Give it a try and just see if it doesn't pull better than your dumb, ole newspaper ad. We'll even write the radio commercial for you at no cost. We've got this young creative genius back at the radio station. Don't worry, he'll work in every one of those copy points you've got in your newspaper ad. I'm telling ya, this guy's a creative genius."

Ask any warrior who ever peddled radio time back in the 50s and he'll tell you that's pretty much how the typical radio sales pitch went. The reason I happen to know, is because I was one of those young creative geniuses back at one of those radio stations.

Every afternoon around the end of the day, one or more of the sales guys would come back to the station and bring me a newspaper ad. "See this ad? Take everything in it and whip it into a radio spot. Gotta be on the air tomorrow at 6:25 a.m. The client wants to make sure you mention "guaranteed lowest prices" three times, "plenty of free parking" twice and "friendly and courteous service" as many times as you can. The more the better, ok?"

Remember the calm, assuring voice of yesteryear's radio commercial? The new voice was now the frenzied delivery of an on-air disc jockey haplessly trying to spit out more words than sixty seconds of time could possibly allow. Commercials didn't speak to listeners, they just yelled at them.

What about the retail advertiser? Well, after being happily assured that every sales point in their newspaper ad had been crammed into the radio commercial, all they had to do was get ready for hoards of buy-happy radio listeners to come tramping into the store the next day.

When the next day came and nobody came happily tramping in, that was pretty much it for radio's over sell and the comparative test.

Not long thereafter, whenever approached by someone in radio sales, former one-time retail radio advertisers would instinctively cower and mutter a woeful lament, that still reverberates today. "Radio's no good good good. We tried it once once once. And it doesn't work work work."

Is there an echo in here?

Chapter 4

Why Can't a Radio Commercial Work like a Newspaper Ad?

When comparing radio listening to newspaper reading, it's apparent that different dynamics are at work in each medium. It is, to borrow a phrase, like comparing apples and oranges. One is listened to while the other is read. One medium requires ears the other needs eyes and, of course, television needs both.

When considering why one chooses to be either a listener or reader, the differences between radio and newspaper become even more apparent.

If a person wanted to hear some music, it is unlikely that they would pick up a newspaper and read the entertainment section. If one wanted to read the comics, find out their horoscope, check on some used-car buys, do a cross-word puzzle or cut out some grocery coupons, it's not likely that they would turn on the radio. When one reads the newspaper, that person's focus and attention is on doing little else, the least of which is driving one's car. When one is listening to the radio, that person is likely to also be focused on doing one or more of several things, like driving one's car. Of course, one can be listening to the radio and reading the newspaper both at the same time, but the focus and attention would apparently be on the newspaper.

It seems safe to conclude that radio is the one medium that is obliged to try harder to gain a significant share of the listener's divided attention or fragmented focus. Obviously then, a radio commercial must try even harder.

While radio commercials and newspaper ads are both intended to motivate the listener or reader to buy or use a given product or service, each one goes about trying to achieve this objective in it's own way. An advertiser, therefore, should not expect that a radio commercial and a newspaper ad will each perform in exactly the same manner or produce the same results. Let's discuss some of the reasons why they won't.

An ad in the newspaper can obviously be read, but it can also be studied. It can be put aside and by choice, perused and referenced again later. A commercial on the radio can't. It can be heard again later, but it's not by choice, it's by chance. When a radio commercial is heard, the listener does not have the option to study and re-examine it. A commercial on the radio vanishes into thin air, while an ad in the newspaper sticks around as long as the newspaper does.

Few, if any listeners ever turn on the radio for the sole purpose of hearing commercials. Nobody really does that. As a matter of fact, after turning on the radio, few care to even hear commercials. It is fundamentally important for advertisers to understand that people turn on the radio for one reason only and that's to listen to the radio. They do not do so in eager anticipation of hearing what advertisers have to say.

Commercials, for the most part, are regarded as obligatory and annoying interruptions. Listeners have been conditioned to patiently endure commercials, often hearing clusters of them over a period of several minutes. Listeners accept radio commercials because they are under no obligation to listen to them. There is no law against not listening.

An ad, on the other hand, is seldom regarded as an intrusion in the newspaper, because, unlike a radio commercial, a newspaper ad really doesn't get in the way of anything, other than helping to bulk up the paper. Ads are something that the reader can simply ignore and just skip by.

Let's hypothetically say that a radio listener wanted to buy some shark repellent and was interested in hearing a commercial about where to buy some. Granted, this point is slightly exaggerated, but it is not likely that the listener would manage to hear such a commercial while they were listening to the radio. Even if such a commercial was aired during this time, it is also likely that this listener wouldn't hear it, because they might be focused on something else, such as talking on a cellphone while rear-ending the car in front of them.

Radio listeners do not search out commercials for specific products or services that they are currently interested in at the moment. There are even significant numbers of radio listeners, at any given time, who are not interested in any of the products or services being advertised on the radio.

When a radio commercial does air, however, it stands alone for thirty or sixty seconds in a spotlight with nothing competing for it's attention, other than what may be preoccupying the individual listener. During this time, the advertiser has an incredible opportunity to not only be heard, but to be listened to by everyone who is listening to that radio station at that moment. It is within the advertiser's creative power to then, amuse, delight, inform, convince and otherwise, make a favorable impression on each and everyone of these listeners, with regard to the product being advertised. There is a caveat, however, as there is no guarantee that all, or even any, of the radio listeners will listen to what's in the spotlight. If the radio commercial is dull, foolish or irritating, the listener can simply dial it out, by not paying attention; turning down the volume; switching to another station; or merely turning the radio off. It's that easy for the listener not to listen.

An advertiser should never presume that everyone listening to the radio, is waiting to hear their commercial, and that hearing and listening are synonymous. Hearing is one thing and listening is quite another.

PERSON #1: Did you hear what I said?

PERSON #2: Yeah. I heard what you said.

PERSON #1: Well, what did I say?

PERSON #2: I don't know, I wasn't listening.

By chance, there may be a segment of listeners who will hear the commercial and choose to listen, for the simple reason that they are indeed, actively interested in the product or service being advertised, like a store that sells shark repellent. Some or perhaps all of this small segment of listeners will respond to the commercial, no matter how mundane or annoying it may be. This may explain why even really bad radio commercials do manage to occasionally generate some immediate, but only short-term results.

Even so, a store shouldn't bank on hoards of people tromping in right after one airing of the commercial. Nor should the store count on the commercial convincing anyone to buy their shark repellent, if the listener is not in need of it. Let's see what the store can count on though.

If they have aired listener-friendly radio commercials that have made favorable and lasting impressions, and these commercials have been supported with enough frequency, then sooner or later large numbers of those listeners will ultimately become customers. After all, ultimately everybody's going to need some shark repellent, right?

With respect to this consideration, two questions are invariably asked "How long is *ultimately?*" and "Can, or will, the advertiser commit to consistently advertising on radio that long?" With rare exception, the answers are "Too long" and "No."

Now let's look at the newspaper ad. Unlike listening to the radio, when people read the newspaper, they often do search out ads for specific products they are currently interested in, like shark repellent.

These readers, sometimes in sizable numbers, are the ones most apt to respond to the newspaper ad, thereby accounting for the advertiser's next-day results. This is exactly what reinforces the retail advertiser's contention that newspaper is more effective than radio.

That's the good news, now here's some newspaper bad news: The rest of the newspaper readers, about 99.7% of them, whom we can call the not interested in shark repellent at the moment readers, are probably not even going to notice the ad in the newspaper. This is what is known as "huge waste circulation."

The figure just quoted, 99.7%, is only a hunch and should not be construed as a scientifically tested hypothesis. If you'd care to go out on your own and sample a cross section of typical newspaper readers, you might find that only 98.4% are not interested in shark repellent at the moment.

Just remember, the smaller and less diverse the sample, the greater the chance of sampling-error. "Sampling-error," means drawing the wrong conclusion about the total population based upon your sample. So don't go out there and just willy-nilly survey a hand full of scuba divers, ok?

With respect to all mediums, there are significant numbers of listeners, viewers and readers, whom I refer to as "product ambivalent ad-watchers." Much like people-watchers, the ad-watchers seem to casually enjoy scrutinizing advertising for no other reason than the advertising just happens to be there in front of them.

What effect any advertiser's message may have on this population, no matter how creative the advertising may be, is anybody's guess.

When it comes to targeting specific audience demographics, with respect to age, sex, education, income, ethnic origin and so forth, radio is significantly more effective than newspaper.

Let's say that Mr. Shark Repellent determined that the best prospects were males between the ages of 24 and 48 with an average of two years of college and annual incomes of forty to seventy thousand dollars.

Depending upon the size of the market and the number of radio stations, he would be able to choose from one or more radio stations which could deliver significant numbers of listeners in that desired audience demographic. Radio is an excellent medium for targeting. To loosely target the same demographic in the newspaper, Mr. Shark Repellent would more than likely, run his ad in the sports section.

When you come right down to it though, if shark repellent is all this retailer has to sell, surely he'd be better off running a few ads once in a while in a magazine like *Shark World Monthly.* On second thought, maybe he'd be better off just going into some other kind of business.

Chapter 5

Yours Truly, the Creative Genius

In the late 1950s, I got my first job in a field in which I thought I might want to pursue a career. It was an entry-level position at a radio station in Portland, Oregon, KEX Radio 1190.

KEX was a top-forty music and personality station and was the number-one rated station in the market. So were all the others, but I think KEX really was. I was even given a title "the assistant to the assistant program director." My official duties were to be of assistance to the assistant program director, as well as anybody else who needed assistance, including the assistant janitor. Additionally, I was expected to be ready to put on my "creative genius hat" at a moments notice.

It was a hat that I wore quite often. One minute I'd be asked to dream up a clever phrase for an on-air promo, like "Be sure to stay tuned for *The Russ Conrad Show.*" The next minute I'd be crafting some well-chosen words for a lively community-service announcement like "The Women's

Auxiliary of The Hail Fellows Well Met will hold their annual pancake-off and rummage sale this Sunday 10am to 4pm in the civic auditorium parking lot." That one is my all time favorite.

The really important thing that I did at the radio station though, happened just about every day late in the afternoon. It was writing live-copy radio commercials. The challenging part was to work in "friendly service," "plenty of free parking," and "guaranteed lowest prices" as many times as possible, as well as all the other copy points, while making sure that the commercial "doesn't sound rushed."

For some reason, no matter who the advertiser was—a car dealer, a furniture store or a pizza parlor—their main selling propositions all seemed to be "friendly service, plenty of free parking and guaranteed lowest prices."

Somehow, the idea of making a career out of writing this kind of radio advertising, didn't seem like anything I'd care to be doing for the rest of my life.

During those rather bleak days, the retail advertisers' idea of a radio commercial was nothing more than a verbatim adaptation of their newspaper ad. That was exactly how the radio sales people encouraged them to use radio. A radio commercial was nothing more than an audio clone of a retail advertiser's newspaper ad, and it was more or less the same with TV.

On the national level, radio had dropped down several preferential rungs on the media ladder, becoming what was and often still is, referred to as a "support medium." The creative mission of a radio commercial was to support the television advertising with the same concept, but without the pictures. The rationale was that these radio commercials would remind listeners of the commercials that they were all presumably seeing on TV. At many advertising agencies today, they still reason that's what radio commercials should do.

One day at the radio station, while trying to come up with a different creative spin for "Be sure to stay tuned for *The Russ Conrad Show*," I heard a radio commercial that actually compelled me to listen.

Immediately, I recognized it as the creative work of Stan Freberg, the celebrated humorist and Capitol recording artist. Freberg is sometimes referred to as "vintage radio's last star."

"What's this? Stan Freberg is now doing radio commercials?" Indeed he was.

The commercial was for Contadina tomato paste and was by no means the run-of-the-mill kind of radio commercial that I had been accustomed to hearing.

First, it was humorous: professionally humorous. It was something nobody had really heard much in radio commercials before. Second, the voices, Stan Freberg and Peter Leeds, as well as the announcer, Bill Baldwin, were outstanding Hollywood professionals. "At last," I thought, "here's an honest-to-goodness, listener-friendly radio commercial, compelling me to listen to it and enjoy listening to it."

Simply, it was just two guys talking, not yelling or screaming mind you, just talking. It was like eavesdropping in on a conversation, but a very humorous one. The humor had all been deftly woven together with the selling message, leaving the listener with a very positive and memorable impression of Contadina. As a matter of fact, the listener was left with the impression that they hadn't even been listening to a commercial. What a welcome and much needed respite from the mindless barrage of "commercial-commercials" I was constantly hearing, but not really listening to all day long. Even the Contadina slogan and jingle was delightful and fresh, "Who puts eight great tomatoes in that little bitty can?"

Today, a radio commercial featuring a couple of professional voice talents engaged in a humorous dialogue, certainly wouldn't come off sounding that unusual or earth shattering. But back in the mid 50s, that sort of repartee in a radio commercial was, what in current advertising jargon, might be called "cutting edge."

After hearing it, I didn't exactly drop everything and rush out to buy a can of Contadina tomato paste. But I can truthfully say that whenever I find myself in need of tomato paste, which isn't that often, Contadina is the brand I look for in the market. How's that for a radio commercial making a memorable, favorable and long-lasting impression?

Soon, I began hearing and listening to more Freberg commercials for other products. Each time I was getting more excited about the creative possibilities of radio advertising. Then one day I decided that was what I wanted to do. Specifically, I wanted to write humorous radio commercials for Stan Freberg. But how? Well, it just meant quitting my job at the radio station in Portland and heading to Los Angeles. It also meant that once there, I had to find a way to meet Stan Freberg and then somehow convince him to hire me. To make the proverbial long story short, I did exactly all of the above, and nearly a year later I was at work in Hollywood, writing humorous radio commercials for Freberg Ltd.

During the two years there, I worked creatively with Freberg on radio campaigns for Zee bathroom tissues, Butternut coffee, Bubble Up, Esskay meats and Kaiser aluminum foil, among others. I look back on it as an enjoyable education and an important creative experience, as well as having the satisfaction that I was playing a part in a newly energized direction in the creation and production of radio commercials.

A new creative standard had been set for radio advertising, and Stan Freberg was the standard bearer. Soon, a few other Los Angeles-based creative radio mavericks joined the ranks of an emerging creative cottage industry, providing outside creative radio commercial services to advertising agencies and their advertiser clients throughout the country. Collectively, this entertaining approach to radio advertising soon became known as "West Coast Radio."

Notably, these Hollywood-based companies were Freberg Ltd., my own newly formed Klein/Barzman, (with former Freberg gm., Bob Klein) Chuck Blore & Don Richmond Creative Services, Mel & Noel Blanc's Blanc Communications, Dallas William's Spot Makers and Bea Shaw Productions. Other early creative radio commercial notables were Walt Kramer's Imagination, Inc. in San Francisco and Fred Arthur in Denver.

In the 1970s, Dick Orkin and Bert Berdis's company, Dick & Bert, in Chicago, made waves in the radio world with their award-winning radio commercials for *Time* magazine, which they did through Young & Rubicam in New York. These commercials were instrumental in helping advertising agencies take serious note of the valuable contributions that outside creative radio resources could make to their clients'radio advertising.

In the 1980s, Craig Wiese, a long-time creative director at Campbell Mithun Advertising in Minneapolis, and rare agency person who actually loved doing radio, started his own creative radio commercial company.

In 1985, Joy Golden, a New York advertising agency print copywriter all of her professional life, took on a freelance assignment to write and produce a series of radio commercials for Laughing Cow cheese. The spots were so well received and acclaimed that Ms. Golden then opened shop as Joy Radio.

In 1982, shortly after the breakup of Dick and Bert, Dick Orkin started his own company, Dick Orkin's Radio Ranch. Bert Berdis and my firm Barzman and Company, along with Jim Kirby, then teamed up as Bert, Barz & Kirby in Los

Angeles. A few years later, Jim Kirby left to start Jim Kirby and Company. Until 1992, Bert Berdis and I were Bert & Barz & Company, then Bert became Bert Berdis & Company and I went back out on my own as BarzRadio.

Back in the 70s/80s, Jerry Stiller and Ann Meara in New York were winning raves and awards for, among others, their continuing series of delightful Blue Nun wine commercials. Likewise, Anne Winn and Garret Brown were receiving kudos for their Molsen commercials. So much so, they were often referred to as "The Molsen Couple."

Creative radio commercial companies flourish in other countries too; Griffith, Gibson & Ramsey in Vancouver, Pirate Radio in Toronto, Street Remely in Adelaide, Australia, and Hobo Radio in London. Other companies offering their creative radio commercial services include, April Winchell's Radio Savant, World Wide Wadio, Sarley Bigg & Bedder, Radio in the Nude and Christopher Barzman's Ferocious Radio, all in Los Angeles. There's Oink-Ink and No Soap Radio in New York. There's Dave Lewis in Chicago. There's the venerable Mal Sharpe in Berkley, California, well-known for his tongue-in-cheek man-on-the-street interviews with real people. There's also John Crawford in San Francisco, and Bart Smith in Seattle. There are others too, whom I'm sure I've neglected to mention and to whom I apologize for neglecting to mention.

As early as the mid 1950s, radio comedy personalities Bob Elliot and Ray Goulding, better known as Bob and Ray were also blazing new comedy trails in radio advertising. Their series of Bert and Harry Piels' beer commercials are invariably mentioned whenever the subject of humorous radio commercials comes up.

Of all the memorable radio spots, one in particular is probably referenced more than any. It was written and produced in the 1960s for the Radio Advertising Bureau by

Freberg Ltd. and was designed to promote radio on radio to the advertising industry. The commercial features the voices of Stan Freberg and the late Paul Frees.

MAN: Radio? Why should I advertise on Radio? There's nothing to look at. No pictures.

FREBERG: Listen, you can do things on radio you couldn't possibly do on TV.

MAN: That'll be the day.

FREBERG: Alright, watch this. (clears throat) Ok people, now when I give you the cue, I want the 700 foot mountain of whipped cream to roll into Lake Michigan, which has been drained and filled with hot chocolate. Then the Royal Canadian Air Force will fly overhead, towing a 10-ton maraschino cherry, which will be dropped into the whipped cream to the cheering of 25,000 extras. Alright, cue the mountain!

SFX: Massive rumbling then huge splash

FREBERG: Cue the air force!

SFX: Airplanes drone

FREBERG: Cue the maraschino cherry!

SFX: Long whistle and dull splash

FREBERG: Okay 25,000 cheering extras!

SFX: Enormous crowd roar

FREBERG: Now, you want to try that on television?

MAN: Well. . . .

FREBERG: You see, radio's a very special medium because it stretches the imagination.

MAN: Doesn't television stretch the imagination?

FREBERG: Up to 21 inches, ye-e-s.

Considering that this commercial was done back in the 1960s, about the only thing that dates it, is that television screens now come in larger sizes.

What this commercial humorously illustrates is the limitless visual possibilities of radio. Pictures and images that each listener can imagine and see merely by listening to words and sound effects.

When Freberg exclaims, "Now, you want to try that on television," he's alluding to the elaborate TV production details and staggering costs it would take to drain Lake Michigan, fill it with hot chocolate and move a mountain of whip cream into it while 25,000 cheering extras stand by as the Royal Canadian Air Force flies overhead and drops a 10-ton maraschino cherry into the whipped cream.

My friend Bill Bratkowski, formerly a partner in Coppos Films, a Los Angeles commercial television production company, suggested that to turn this radio commercial into a TV commercial wouldn't be that difficult. "All of those production elements," he said, "could be shot with miniatures and computer graphics." When I asked him to guess what those costs might be, he thought for a moment and said, "Well, considerably more than what they were for the radio spot."

The visuals of radio and its power to stimulate the imagination is no more vividly illustrated than in the famous Orson Welles Mercury Theater radio production, *War of the Worlds,* which was heard on Halloween eve, October 30, 1938. Here's some of what was reported in the *New York Times* the next day.

A wave of mass hysteria seized thousands of radio listeners throughout the nation between 8:15 and 9:30 last night when a broadcast of a dramatization of

H.G. Wells fantasy, *The War of the Worlds,* led thousands to believe that an interplanetary conflict had started with invading Martians spreading wide death and destruction in New Jersey and New York. The broadcast, which disrupted households, created traffic jams and clogged communications systems, was made by Orson Welles. . . .at least a score of adults required medical treatment for shock and hysteria.

Radio's wondrous ability, is to seat the listener front row center and present the kind of visual programming that raises the curtain on each person's individual theater of the imagination. By and large, that curtain has come down, as radio's "theater of the imagination" is pretty much dark.

Hold on, there's still those frequent one-minute interludes—you remember, commercials? What about working in some theater of the imagination into them? Who knows, people might even listen.

Chapter 6

Once Outside the Pit

One of the really swell memories I have as a young kid was the episodic excitement of the late afternoon radio serial programs.

We'd all be outside playing Kick the Can, Hide and Go Seek, or Annie Annie Over, when suddenly someone would shout "Hey, look what time it is!" Everybody would clear out and make a mad dash for home. That's when our favorite serial radio adventure programs were on. And boy, did the writers of these episodic serial adventures have a field day with our young, little minds. "Be sure to join us next time boys and girls, when we'll find out if our hero gets out of this harrowing situation alive."

Who were they kidding? No matter how harrowing, we always knew that our hero would somehow manage to get out. However, the one thing we never knew was just exactly how. Speculating about it was all part of the fun. After each episode we'd gather and have spirited discussions about how the pending escape would unfold.

"Maybe there's a secret trap door. . . ." "Too obvious." "I know, he gets swooped up and carried away by a tornado."

"Not a chance." And even if we thought that we had figured it out, it always turned out that we were wrong.

Eventually these episodic serial adventures made their way to the silver screen in the form of weekly Saturday morning or afternoon matinees. Making their way to the theaters in droves, were all those prepubescent, young radio fans.

Every Saturday, hundreds of excited kids with their quarters and box tops in hand, would line up in front of neighborhood theaters all across the land, to find out how their favorite hero would get out of the mess that he was left in last week.

One such episode had our hero dashing through the jungle. I don't really recall if he was being chased or if he was doing the chasing. Suddenly, some jungle fauna underfoot gave way and our hero abruptly tumbled down into a cavernous pit.

Naturally he was ok, but as soon as he stood up in the bottom of this pit, he found that he was ankle deep in gooey slime. To make matters worse, it was slowly oozing from every crack and crevice in the walls surrounding the pit. Shades of Indiana Jones?

No theater of the imagination necessary here, as it was graphically apparent that getting out of this slimy pit was going to be near impossible. The pending consequence was clear. If our hero didn't get out soon, or at least by next week's episode, he was certain to die a most improbable death by drowning in this gooey slime that was slowly inching up and approaching his knees.

Of course, we were all confident that he'd manage to get out, but we also knew that only the writer really knew how.

One week later, we found out that our hero, indeed, got out of the pit. What we didn't find out, was how. As the episode began, we heard the announcer simply say "Once outside the pit." That was it, he was out. To the hoots, hollers and whistles of the delighted young audience, our hero was then blithely off on a new adventure.

As for the searching question "How exactly did he get out of the pit?" Well, as they might have suggested in Creative Radio Writing 101, "That's something best left to the imagination." Of course, that could also suggest that the writer couldn't figure it out either.

Chapter 7

Capturing the Listener: A Secret Is Revealed

Early in my professional life, I heard an expert lecture on the subject of radio advertising. Since I had never heard anyone, let alone an expert speak on this subject, I was anxious to hear his pearls of wisdom.

He began his presentation by whetting our appetite with the promise of revealing a secret to successful radio commercial making. But first, he prefaced his secret, by saying that a radio commercial must always capture the listener, but before capturing, the commercial must first grab the listener. Then came the secret. According to this self-professed pundit, the secret is to begin the radio commercial with an annoying sound effect, like a clanging bell or a loud buzzer. He said this production technique "will grab the listener's attention," resulting in their capture. "Once captured," he further suggested, "the listener is then putty in the hands of the advertiser." If it were only that simple.

Someone once asked me if I had a definition for a good radio commercial. "Good question," I said, even though I really didn't have an answer. Without giving it any thought, I blurted out, "Sure I do. A good radio commercial? Easy. . . . A good radio commercial is. . . . a radio commercial that uh. . . doesn't really sound uh. . . . like a radio commercial." Sensing that I was on a roll, for good measure I threw in, "And it's certainly one that doesn't start off with the sound of a loud buzzer or clanging bell." That, by the way, has been my official definition ever since.

If an advertiser wants to capture listeners, then their radio commercial shouldn't try to do it by force. The best way to capture listeners is to first captivate them. Once captivated, they may not necessarily be putty in the advertisers hands, but they will certainly be prone to listen to what the advertiser has to say.

Let's now take a look at just exactly what goes into a radio commercial. The basic ingredient is spoken words. In our language there seems to be two different ways people employ spoken words. The first is the way people speak and converse in everyday real life. The second is the way people often abnormally speak and converse in everyday radio commercials, speaking in the gratuitous tongue of "copy point talk." The mistaken presumption that advertisers make is that listeners will become so motivated by being subjected to a continuous plethora of selling information, that they will immediately run out and buy the product.

Nothing makes a radio commercial more unbelievable and such a turn-off, as a dialogue between two people who are merely exchanging copy-points.

Do you suppose that the advertiser responsible for the following commercial, actually believed that anyone was going to listen or even try to process what's being said? (This is an actual radio commercial, only names and locale have been changed to protect the guilty.)

GIRL: What kind of camera do you have there?

GUY: A Panton XR Super. What camera do you have?

GIRL: A Panton E 4000.

SFX: Automatic shutter clicking

GUY: Can I make my camera shoot that fast?

GIRL: Sure, you can get an auto-winder for about a hundred and twenty dollars. But you should do what I did. Trade in your XR Super at Swellshot Camera for a Panton E 4000 and pay only seventy-nine dollars. It's less expensive than an auto-winder and you get a new one-year warranty from Panton. With repairs averaging about sixty dollars, one repair would run almost as much. So you'll save money in the long run too.

GUY: You mean Swellshot Camera will sell me a brand new Panton E 4000. . . .

SFX: More camera clicking

GUY: (continues) for only seventy-nine dollars, plus my XR Super? Great.

GIRL: Sure is. Swellshot Camera is your trade-in headquarters. They do more trade-ins than any other camera store in town. They give better trade-in allowances, too.

GUY: Will they take my Monoxus camera in trade?

GIRL: Yes.

GUY: Limpuss?

GIRL: Yes.

GUY: Zeissfahrt?

GIRL: Yes.

GUY: Sakeshica?

GIRL: Yes. Yes. Yes. Almost any camera. All trade-ins must be in good condition and are subject to inspection. Swellshot Camera, 2496 East Kremmelman Blvd, one block north of Falafels on a Stick. Ample parking. They'll try to meet or beat any locally advertised price.

GUY: Swellshot Camera, huh?

I have never seen any documentation suggesting that the more sales information and product hyperbole there is in a radio commercial, the more that correlates with a commercial's ultimate effectiveness. Quite the opposite is true. A radio commercial is much more listenable and effective when it highlights or emphasizes only one or two salient sales or copy points and then leaves itself enough room to creatively expand from there.

As was suggested earlier, a lot of specific and detailed sales information can be included in a newspaper ad because the reader can leisurely read, re-read and study the information.

In a radio commercial, however, in one fell swoop all of the information comes fleetingly flying out of the radio. The listener doesn't have the luxury of rewinding and re-listening to the commercial. Once it is presented, it's gone. The listener may hear it again by chance, or perhaps not.

No matter how well intentioned, many advertisers can't resist the temptation to cram as much copy and ad verbiage as possible into their radio commercial. I suppose they figure that if they're paying for all of that radio time, then they're darned well going to use every last second's worth to pitch what they're selling.

I don't believe that radio commercials should be designed just for the client's approval alone. It's equally, if not more, important, that they be designed for the listeners' approval as well.

Granted, the advertiser is the one paying for the commercial, but the advertiser isn't the one who's going to be hearing it. If those hearing the commercial don't care or choose to listen to it, then what's the advertiser paying for?

A Radio Commercial: Writing It and Presenting It

A large Chicago advertising agency once hired me to produce and direct a radio commercial, which was written by one of their copywriters, who, along with an account executive, flew out to Los Angeles to be at the recording session. The commercial was for a breakfast cereal and was written to highlight the point that there were "four apples in every box."

Conceptually, the commercial was based upon William Tell ineptly trying to shoot apples off of his son's head with a bow and arrow. The part of William Tell was voiced by actor/comedian Tom Poston, and his young son was played by my son, Christopher Barzman. The announcer was Bill Ratner.

Midway through the commercial, after several bow and arrow misses, including breaking a window and hitting a cow, the announcer suggests to William Tell that a box of our cereal with four apples in it would make "a nice big target." William Tell rhetorically exclaims "four apples?" Then shouts, "Here son, put this box on your head." In the distance we hear the son as he catches the box say "ok." William says to the announcer, "Now hand me three more arrows," and we then hear the son whimper "Oh no." As we hear the sound of four successive arrows being slung, the announcer's voice comes over the sound with the closing product sell, and the commercial has ended.

During the recording session we found that each read or "take" of the commercial was coming up short. In other words, even after allowing four or five seconds for the sound effects, which would bring the commercial out to about fifty-nine seconds, the reads were all ending at around fifty seconds. It was apparent that we needed to pad the text with about four more seconds of verbiage.

It was also apparent that the commercial really didn't have an ending or a payoff. As it was, it just concluded rather flatly on the announcer's product sell line "with four apples in every box." What this commercial seemed to cry out for was some kind of humorous resolution of this William Tell bow and arrow concept.

We decided to do another take, this time with the idea of coming up with a much needed humorous resolution. Instead of hastily trying to write something, I suggested to the writer that we see what happens if we ask Tom Poston (William Tell) to ad lib about four seconds after the announcer's concluding speech.

Tom ad-libbed, (Shouting) "Did I hit the apples son?" There was then a brief moment of silence and he yelled out again, "Son?" There was even time to add a pastoral second or two of birds twittering. Now the commercial was over.

The writer and I, even the recording engineer really liked the way the commercial ended now; it was funny.

Then the account fellow, who all during the session had been pensively sitting in a corner of the control booth, spoke up "Wait a minute, he said scratching his head, what's the client gonna say about this?" "Say about what?" I innocently asked. "About this new ending. I mean, I'm not sure how the client is gonna feel about William Tell killing his son." "Killing his son?" I queried. "You know, with the bow and arrow," he said. "Woah, hold on," I said. "Where did you get the idea that William Tell killed his son? He didn't kill him. He just dazed him. See, those arrows had rubber tips." I looked over at the writer and he nodded in affirmation. "Yeah," he said, "rubber tips." "Oh," the rather befuddled account executive said, "well, if he was just dazed by the arrows, then I guess that's ok. Yeah, I don't think that the client will have a problem with this new ending."

On the subject of writing radio commercials, a question that's often asked is "How or where do you get your ideas?" As was just illustrated, some of the best ideas come up as spontaneous creative after-thoughts right there during the recording session. Client advertisers and the advertising agency production teams should always encourage and be receptive to good spontaneous ideas that can serve to plus the commercial they're making.

As for me, and I'm sure for most advertising writers, the whole creative hunting and gathering process begins with the product. In any product or service there inevitably lies the seed of something unique, pertinent or peculiar to that product or service. Often it's something that has come out of consumer research and is tucked somewhere in the sales and marketing objective. A good idea could even come from something about the competition's product or service. Contrary to popular notion, it seldom, if ever, comes to the writer while taking a shower.

This seed of something is often difficult to put your finger on, or it's seemingly not there at all, but it's there. The really good and original ideas are not usually the obvious ones. The obvious ideas are usually the creative inclinations to try to avoid. It's important that the writer objectively ask themself, "is the idea that I'm thinking about here, something that any number of other copywriters might come up with?" If the answer is "yes," then the idea is probably trite.

Once found, the truly unexpected idea can translate into a unique premise for an arresting commercial, or series of commercials, that are quantum-leap creative cuts above the rest. Good creative directors are those who, in the early concept stage, recognize unique ideas and encourage their writers to develop these creative inclinations.

The idea of William Tell trying to shoot apples and then a box of breakfast cereal off of his son's head is not especially brilliant or terribly original. It is, however, a good example of a creative concept, gleaned from a sales and marketing proposition uniquely pertinent to that product: "Four Apples in Every Box." It does therefore, get an *A* in my book for creatively being on target. On second thought, with Tom Poston's ad lib ending, let's make that an *A plus.*

The skill of writing, the finesse of presenting and the craft of directing and producing, are ostensibly three separate stages in the evolution of a radio commercial. They should, however, be regarded as interrelated steps in a singular process. The way the process often goes at advertising agencies is like the way a relay race is run.

A copywriter takes the first lap by writing the commercial. The script is then handed off to an account person who dashes over to the client and presents it. Once approved, the script is slapped into the hands of an agency producer, who sprints to the finish line and produces it.

This tag team approach is not the most efficient or effective way to put radio commercials together. The pivotal person in the process is the writer. The writer is the logical one to present and explain the radio commercial to the client.

Where humor is concerned, there are often nuances of interpretation, delivery and timing, which at the script stage may only be apparent to the writer. These subtleties are not always apparent to the client, especially when they are merely handed the script of the commercial and asked to read it.

Even worse is when an account executive is obliged to put on an actor hat and then perform the commercial for the client; it is usually not a pretty sight.

In either case, the client is likely to be disinterested, perusing the script or gazing out the window, while taking mental note of nothing more than how often the product's name or "ample parking" is mentioned. Invariably, the client will conclude that the commercial "Isn't on target" or "It just doesn't grab me."

Obviously, the best person to present a radio commercial script is the writer. However, if the writer happens to be shy or uncomfortable in the presence of the client, then another presentation plan needs to be put in place.

An excellent presentation strategy is to hire some professional voice talents and record a demo of the commercial in a recording studio. This demo will most accurately indicate to the client the intended sound and character of the commercial. Often there is a fine line between a demo and the finished the commercial. It is not uncommon for a demo to actually go to air as the finished radio commercial. Visual presentation materials, such as layouts, storyboards and animatics, rarely, if ever, end up as the final creative product.

The manner in which radio commercial scripts are presented to clients is an important step in the making of a radio commercial. This presentation phase is, so to speak, the point of return or no return. If rejected, it means a return to the drawing board and then a return to present something else to the client. If approved, it means "no return," and that's the green light to proceed with the recording and production of the finished commercial. It could even mean that the demo is "good for go" just as is, or perhaps it just means a quick return to the studio to re-record a new line and tweak the demo.

I am reminded of an evening once when I was in attendance at a gala advertising affair in New York. Several hundred advertising people were there, resplendent in their tuxedos and gowns, milling about during the social cocktail hour. I too was milling, but not so resplendent in my hastily rented tuxedo. Soon I became engaged in a conversation with a man who was apparently a super-senior-extremely-important-executive-vice-president at a major New York advertising agency. At least, that was more or less what was on his business card.

After giving me his card, plus the details of his meteoric rise in the advertising world, he asked what I did. When I told him that I wrote and produced humorous radio commercials, he cringed and took two steps backwards.

"Anything wrong?" I asked. "Radio," he snarled with contempt, "I hate radio. We never do radio at our agency." "Never?" I said, "for none of your clients?" "None," he replied, "never, it's agency policy." I strongly sensed that he wanted to be done with our conversation and continue milling, so I said, "Well, it's been nice chatting with you, and oh, just out of curiosity, what is it exactly that your agency doesn't like about radio?" This is what he said, "When you're in a meeting and you play radio spots for the client, the client never knows what to look at. It's extremely awkward and uncomfortable." He then walked away.

It's a good thing that we weren't seated at the same table at dinner. No doubt I would have flung my tomato aspic at him and a food fight would have ensued.

Often in an agency/client relationship, a great divide exists between the client advertiser and the people at the source of the creative work. This divide occurs when the creative people have never interacted with the client people. In spite of a neutral buffer zone usually manned and patrolled by account people, a relationship void like this can have a negative impact on the final creative product.

If there's not a mutual understanding in terms of the creative direction, then what can result is disappointment, frustration and even suspicion. This is usually the case when the creative people find themselves especially enamored with what they have just created for presentation, but the client people don't share their "enamorization."

From the creative perspective, there's frustration and disappointment that the client is too rigid or square or simply "just doesn't get it." From the client's perspective, there's disappointment that the creative people are off base or suspicion that maybe they're all "smoking something."

Before the creative process even begins, it's important for client and creative to be on the same wave length. Not just in terms of the sales and marketing strategy, but also in terms of the advertising's creative tenor and style.

Even so, how often have creative people, after presenting their scripts or concepts, heard their client say, "that's not what I had in mind." Client advertisers should recognize that creative people are not, by nature, psychics or mind readers. When a client does "have something in mind," they should make an effort to spell it out. However, once delineated, the client should not presume or expect that their "creative vision" is necessarily going to be happily embraced by the agency creatives.

I am told of a client presentation meeting, where after rejecting all of the radio scripts the agency team had presented, the client then told the agency team his ideas for the radio commercials, and instructed them to script those. Respectfully, the creative director suggested to the client that perhaps it would be best if he, the client simply wrote these radio commercials himself. To which the client replied, "If I knew how do it myself, then I wouldn't need you."

I've always thought that would make a nice title for a book.

Chapter 9

Humor

When a radio commercial is regarded as being creative, it's nearly always humorous. Perhaps that's why, in the categories of radio at creative advertising awards shows, so many of the favorite winning commercials are usually the humorous ones.

If a writer is not especially skilled or comfortable creating humor, does this preclude that person from doing creative radio commercials? Not at all, and I'll go into that later.

There are many advertisers who seem leery and are even afraid of humor in their radio advertising. I once got a call from a small advertising agency inquiring about my services to create a radio commercial for one of their clients. The call came from the owner of the agency who began by saying, "We're familiar with your work and think it's very good and we'd like you to do a radio commercial for one of our bank clients, but this client doesn't like humor."

Hold on. Did I hear correctly? His client doesn't like humor? So why is this agency, who thinks my work is very good, calling me then? Before responding, I thought for a brief moment, "Get a grip here and be careful what you say."

I wanted to say, "How does this bank client feel about Air? Food? Sex? What do you mean he doesn't like humor? Has your client never laughed? Chortled? Guffawed? What about jokes? Has he never told or heard one? Has this client of yours not ever read an amusing article, book or seen a funny movie or play? How 'bout television? Doesn't he watch it? Has he never seen *Seinfeld* or *Saturday Night Live?* Does he read *New Yorker* magazine and ignore the cartoons? What's with this client of yours who doesn't like humor?"

Then it dawned on me. It's not that the client personally doesn't like humor, it's that he doesn't want any humor in his bank's advertising. Perhaps he feels that humor might interfere or overwhelm their sales message. I know what it is: Humor would be inappropriate and make light of the importance and dignity of their bank.

After all, there's nothing funny about money, right? This is serious stuff. Heaven forbid, what if the humor backfired? If that happened, there'd be such a run on the bank that it would be more catastrophic than the rush of the Great Depression. Do we want to take that risk all for some funny, little radio commercials? Not on your free unlimited check-writing checking account!

As you may be gathering, I didn't do a commercial for them. Not only did they not want to do anything humorous, but it also turned out that that the bank was a little short on funds, so they couldn't pay much of anything for a radio commercial. I told the agency owner that if his client ever changed his mind about doing a radio commercial with a little humor, then I'd take up a collection. He thought that was very funny.

As for humor backfiring, let me assure you that it doesn't. In the annals of radio advertising, I know of no instance when masses of listeners ever boycotted any product or service because of humorous radio commercials.

What does happen once in a while though, is that someone will conclude that there is something about the commercial's humor that's offensive to them. This type of person is most likely to write letters to the advertiser and/or the advertising agency and/or even the radio stations. They may even register their complaint with a phone call, fax or e-mail. This, however, should not be a source of great concern for the advertiser. Advertisers should know, and therefore expect, that when doing humorous radio commercials there is a good chance that somebody's going to come out of the woods with a chip on their shoulder.

Shortly after my former partners and I formed Bert, Barz & Kirby in the early 1980s, we were engaged by Compton Advertising in New York to create and produce a series of radio commercials for their client, Paine Webber.

Paine Webber is a well known and highly respected stock brokerage company with offices throughout the country. Humor was something that they weren't against doing on radio, but they were a little concerned about how we'd go about creatively handling it in their commercials. The people at the agency put it this way, "We'd like you to do some funny commercials for our client but not too funny."

We were told that in terms of demographics, these commercials would be aimed at a more affluent audience of adult listeners, specifically targeted to those with sizable disposable incomes. The media buy was placed on radio stations most likely to reach those listeners (i.e. classical, jazz, oldies and news and talk stations.)

These radio commercials would be running on the heels of their recent and highly visible "Thank You Paine Webber" television campaign, so we were asked, for the sake of thematic continuity, to creatively design the commercials to incorporate that line. We were also asked to use the same announcer copy-block from the television commercials as well. "In this highly competitive financial world, Paine Webber believes the quality of life just might depend upon the quality of your investments." This line was delivered by the late, distinguished actor Burgess Meredith, who was Paine Webber's spokesperson.

Based upon this input, we (Bert, Barz & Kirby) wrote and produced several funny, but not too funny, radio spots over the next couple of years. Here is the text of one of them titled "Piano Recital."

MUSIC: SOUR NOTES OF A PIANO BEING POORLY PLAYED IN BACKGROUND

WOMAN #l: (Proudly to woman seated next to her) That's my son playing.

WOMAN #2: (Being polite) Very nice.

WOMAN #1: I taught him myself.

MUSIC: BAD PIANO PLAYING CONCLUDES. LIGHT APPLAUSE

LADY M.C.: Thank you Bobby Chambers. Next on our program, Allison Berdis.

MUSIC: PIANO NOW BEING PLAYED LIKE A VIRTUOSO

WOMAN #1: That's your daughter, isn't it?

WOMAN #2: Yes.

WOMAN #1: She's very talented.

WOMAN #2: Oh, thank you.

WOMAN #1: She plays that piano like she owns one.

WOMAN #2: Thank you, she does.

WOMAN #1: Oh. She plays like she's studied in Europe.

WOMAN #2: Thank you, she has.

WOMAN #1: Oh. How could you. . .?

WOMAN #2: Thank you, Paine Webber.

ANNCR: In this highly competitive financial world, Paine Webber believes the quality of life just might depend upon the quality of your investments.

WOMAN #1: Paine Webber, huh?

WOMAN #2: Yes.

WOMAN #1: Oh I've heard of them . . . they're very good . . . very famous.

WOMAN #2: Yes.

WOMAN #1: Tell me, where can I buy their records?

MUSIC: PIANO CONCLUDES. AUDIENCE APPLAUSE UNDER

ANNCR: Put Paine Webber to work for you. Who knows, you too might say. . . .

YOUNG GIRL: (Acknowledging applause) Thank you. Thank you. And thank *you* Paine Webber.

The reason that I'm referencing this particular commercial is because I feel that it met the parameters of what we were asked to cover, including the "not too funny" part.

Further, I believe that this commercial would've done a fairly good job, if it hadn't been pulled off the air. Oh, I'm sorry, I guess I didn't mention that.

After running on radio stations all over the country for about two weeks, the client suddenly instructed their agency to notify the radio stations to yank the commercial. It seems that our innocent little piano recital offended some people. According to the final tally, about seven or eight, so we were told. Can you guess who we unintentionally offended? No idea? It was a handful of American piano teachers who were miffed enough to write letters, "Where does Paine Webber get off suggesting in their commercial that one has to go to Europe to properly learn how to play the piano? This is an affront to American piano teachers!" Hey lighten up, it's only a radio commercial and a not too funny one at that. The slight was not by design.

Advertisers shouldn't be overly concerned or worry about letters from a few disgruntled radio listeners. Letters of this kind are typically written by those who are neither customers nor prospective ones for the product or service being advertised. They are penned instead, by well intentioned watch dogs of advertising, who are constantly on point to sniff out something to growl about.

Remember the type of radio listeners described earlier? The "product-ambivalent ad watchers?" They are the ones who actively listen to radio commercials simply because they're there. Well, those who write the letters seem to represent the militant fringe.

Advertisers should realize that many of those who write letters make a practice of it, and it is likely that other advertisers too have heard from some of the same people. What should be concluded from these letters is that people are listening to their commercial.

What turns me off of a radio commercial is when the commercial is obviously trying very hard to be funny and it isn't. As Stan Freberg aptly once said, "Humor in the hands of a novice is like a loaded gun in the hands of a child." Creating humor in radio advertising is best left to those who can do it, not to those who just think they can do it.

When it comes to fearing humor, advertisers should work through that fear and understand that there are many different kinds of humor, with undoubtedly a style or genre that's appropriate for them. The humor in a radio commercial for a high-end luxury car, would obviously have a much different character to it, than the humor in a commercial for a chain of whoopee-cushion stores.

So, is there some secret or trick to writing humor for radio? Well sort of, and I'll get into that momentarily. First let's look at the elements the writer has to work with when creating radio commercials. By my calculation there seem to be only four: spoken words, sound effects, music and silence.

Without words there wouldn't be much of a radio commercial. Because there are so many of them, the only tricky thing the writer has to figure out is how these words will be assembled for the commercial. That means coming up with a conceptual structure for the commercial. The simplest way is to assemble the words as a straight-forward sales pitch. This is read as live copy or fact-sheet information by a radio station on-air person and is known as a "live copy" commercial.

If a live copy radio commercial isn't written in the particular style of a specific radio station personality, for delivery by that personality, then it must be written in a generic fashion so that anyone who happens to deliver it can easily and comfortably do so. Other than a few directorial instructions the writer might indicate on the script, there is no control over how those words will be delivered.

This is my least favorite way of doing radio commercials. With few exceptions, live-copy commercials do not result in a very effective use of radio for the advertiser. The only good thing that can be said about doing radio commercials the live-copy way is that the advertiser incurs little or no expense for voice talent and recording studio costs. Saving money on production costs, however, should not be the reason for doing a commercial this way.

Another one-voice option, which is my second least favorite way to do radio commercials, is to create a specific character and tonality for the commercial. This approach usually takes the form of a monologue. An appropriate voice talent is then chosen, usually through an audition or by listening to voice tapes. Once selected, the voice talent is then booked and recorded at a studio prior to the scheduled air date.

By doing a one voice commercial this way, there is directorial input for the voice's interpretation and delivery during the recording session. If appropriate, other production elements, like music and/or sound effects can also be added to the voice track. These elements can contribute to the production values of the commercial by making it a fuller sounding presentation.

A couple of things are worth noting about one-voice commercials, whether they are live-copy or preproduced monologues. When paying the talent is a budgetary issue, a one-voice commercial is obviously less expensive to produce and pay for in terms of session, use and residual fees than multiple-voiced commercials. If not imaginatively scripted and then carefully voiced and produced, however, a one-voice commercial can seemingly drone on for what can feel like a boring eternity. A dialogue between two voices makes for a much more interesting and listenable radio commercial. Three, four or five voices? The more the merrier.

Why even make a radio commercial humorous in the first place? If the advertiser is paying all that money to give people important information about their product, what else do listeners really need to hear? Why should an advertiser be concerned about humor or feel compelled to co-mingle it with his product sell? Is it really necessary to sugar-coat the pill with humor? I believe that it is because when the pill is sugar-coated, more people are apt to swallow it.

Any advertiser can give a writer several good reasons to tell the listener why they should buy their product. However, it's then up to the writer to give the listener one good reason just to listen to their commercial. Humor can be that reason.

Beside being a friendly invitation to listen, humor has other benefits for the advertiser. It can break down barriers between the consumer and the advertiser, making the consumer feel comfortable about buying the product or using the service. Humor can work to help the listener perceive the product or service as being one of quality, integrity and friendliness.

Often when I have directed agency-written radio commercials, I've noticed the words "friendly" or "quality" prominently written into the scripts, as in "Our sales people are friendly," or "Only the finest quality ingredients go into our product." Merely saying it though, doesn't necessarily make it true.

Commercials give advertisers a forum to say seemingly significant things, which are often nothing more than empty claims. "We do it all for you." "Our fresh vegetables are garden grown." "Our breads have that oven-baked goodness." Expressions such as these are intended to tantalize but only serve to water-down the credibility of advertising. This too can be the case with slogans: "Catera. It's the Caddy that Zigs." Try as I will, I've never figured that one out, but I digress.

The perception of a product's quality, or the idea that the advertiser's employees are friendly, is most convincingly expressed through the friendliness and the creative quality of the radio commercial itself. When there is quality in the writing, performances, and production values of the commercial, then what is being advertised will be perceived as one of quality or friendliness. When a product or service is not up to these professed standards, it's misleading and inappropriate to suggest otherwise in the commercial.

The late sage pundit, Bill Bernbach, of the advertising agency Doyle Dane Bernbach, wisely suggested that "nothing can kill a bad product faster than good advertising."

My former company, Bert Barz & Kirby, was once engaged by some people who were in the process of producing and packaging a new dessert topping. This product was similar to an aerosol canned whipped-cream topping, but it wasn't whipped cream, it was whipped yogurt. It was called "Yo Whip."

It was their intention to initially introduce this new product in the Los Angeles market with an awareness radio campaign, which we were to create. If successful, the product would be rolled out nationally.

As we were writing the radio commercials, we were aware that our client was in some rather frenzied throes of trying to line up last-minute distribution for Yo Whip in many of the supermarket chains.

There's an old marketing truism that merely says, "Availability makes sales." If a product isn't adequately distributed and placed on the stores shelves, no one's going to be able to find it, therefore, no one is likely to buy it, no matter how wonderful the advertising. Such was somewhat the case with Yo Whip.

I say "somewhat" because as the radio spots were hitting the Los Angeles air waves, the availability of "Yo Whip" in the supermarkets was somewhat spotty. Many of those who heard the commercials obviously listened, and they were sufficiently motivated to try to find this product.

I'll get back to the "try" part in a moment. Here's one of the commercials.

SFX: RESTAURANT BACKGROUND AMBIANCE UNDER

ANNCR: (Quiet, secretive voice) We're here at world famous Sid and Sally's Steak-a-Rama to conduct an experiment.

PATRON: Uh Sid, is my steak ready yet?

SID: Just about.

ANNCR: We're replacing this customer's 14-ounce medium rare porterhouse steak with this. . . .

SFX: AEROSOL CAN SPRITZ: WHIPPED CREAM "POOF"

ANNCR: Yo Whip . . . the brand new, all natural, whipped yogurt topping and dessert that comes in a can. Let's see if he notices.

SID: Here you go.

SFX: DINNER PLATE CLUNKS DOWN ON TABLE

PATRON: Why thanks. Say, this doesn't look like my usual Sid and Sally's Steak-a-Rama steak Sid. It's white and puffy.

ANNCR: He's talking about french vanilla Yo Whip. Yo Whip also comes in wild strawberry and Bavarian chocolate.

PATRON: Wow. Talk about tender, this steak cuts like whipped cream.

ANNCR: But it's not whipped cream. Yo Whip is whipped yogurt, with 75% less fat and 50% less cholesterol.

PATRON: Mmm. Yummy. I've never tasted a porterhouse as cool and delicious. Why you could put this steak on any pie or fruit or cake.

ANNCR: Or as a snack or dessert, right out of the can.

SID: Ready for dessert?

PATRON: You bet Sid.

ANNCR: Now we've replaced his dessert. . . .

SFX: PIECE OF MEAT SLAPPED ON PLATE

ANNCR: With a 14-ounce porterhouse steak.

SFX: DINNER PLATE CLUNKS DOWN ON TABLE

PATRON: Wait a minute. Is pie á la mode supposed to sizzle like this?

ANNCR: Yo Whip. Better than whipped cream. . . .

SFX: AEROSOL CAN SPRITZ "POOF"

ANNCR: It's yogurt.

For those who did manage to find and then purchase Yo Whip, they were in for a rather unpleasant surprise because it wasn't exactly what the commercials cracked it up to be. It seems that something went awry in the canning process. One might call it a "production quality control glitch."

Instead of that "yummy, cool, delicious," puffy poof you were supposed to get when you gave the can a spritz, what you really got was an oozey dribble. If anyone happened to be counting, there were about three oozey dribbles to the can. At around $2.95 a can, that came to about a buck a dribble.

Needless to say, this product fell flat on it's aerosol can. When a product is devoid of the qualities that it's advertising professes it has, then the advertising can only serve to hasten it's demise. Just as Bill Bernbach suggested.

By the time our company became aware of the problems with this product, the commercials were already airing and we were being informed that we shouldn't expect to get paid. All was not lost however, because we did end up with some excellent examples of our creative radio work and some nice awards.

To those who bought a can of Yo Whip and expected a puffy poof but got an oozey dribble instead, on behalf of my former company, I apologize for the bum steer.

Chapter 10

Who's on First?

Dialogue between two people is the most common way that humor is used in radio commercials. While certainly not unique to radio commercials, dialogue seems to be more prevalent in radio than in television commercials.

The common denominator in any humorous dialogue is conflict. If there is any secret to writing humor, then that's the secret. Without conflict there is seldom humor. So what is meant by "conflict?" Simply, when two characters are at odds, there is conflict.

Abbot & Costello's famous radio baseball routine, "Who's on First?" is a fine example. In the sketch, Abbott is trying to explain to Costello that the players on the St. Louis Wolves baseball team all have peculiar nicknames.

ABBOTT: Now on the team we have Who's on first, What's on second, I Don't Know is on third.

COSTELLO: That's what I want to find out. . . the names of the fellows on the team.

ABBOTT: I'm telling you. Who's on first, What's on second, I Don't Know is on third.

COSTELLO: You know the fellows' names?

ABBOTT: Yes.

COSTELLO: Well then who's playin' first?

ABBOTT: Yes.

COSTELLO: I mean the fellow's name on first base.

ABBOTT: Who.

COSTELLO: Well what are you askin me for?

ABBOTT: I'm not asking you. I'm telling you. Who is on first.

COSTELLO: I don't know.

ABBOTT: He's on third. . . . (and so on).

Conflict exists when one or both of the characters manifest expressions of frustration, contradiction, misunderstanding, disagreement, confusion, chagrin or anger.

For a commercial to be compelling and listenable, conceptually it must have a reason for being, other than to just disseminate information about a product or a service. The characters in the commercial should have the semblance of a life that is not necessarily centered around the product or service. That life should be creatively grounded in who the characters are, as the details of their conflict play out with respect to the product being advertised. If a concept is developed where the characters lives are, indeed, centered around the product or service and there is no conflict, then the characters in the commercial are only existing for the purpose of exchanging copy point and selling information. In short, it's a commercial that is neither listener-friendly or compelling to listen to.

Here's an example of a radio campaign that my company, BarzRadio, recently did for a wireless cable-television company that services the San Bernadino/Riverside area. This area is about sixty miles east of Los Angeles and is known as "The Inland Empire."

The company is Cross Country Wireless Cable and the marketing strategy was two fold: Convince potential cable subscribers that "wireless" cable service, namely Cross Country Wireless, is better and more reasonably priced than regular cable television service; and encourage existing regular cable subscribers to switch to Cross Country Wireless.

This advertiser committed about 90 percent of their advertising budget to radio. During the two-year duration of this radio campaign, we created and produced about thirty different radio commercials. This radio campaign was like an episodic sitcom series.

Conceptually, we created a fictitious cable company "Bumbly Cable." Each episode highlighted the trials and tribulations of this pathetic company, while pointing out the attributes of Cross Country Wireless. The characters were Mr. Bumbly, the inept and bombastic owner, Miss Potter, Mr. Bumbly's all-knowing and acerbic assistant, and Felix, Mr.Bumbly's incompetent and dorky nephew. I assayed the role of Mr. Bumbly and Patti Deutsch and Eddie Deezan were respectively Miss Potter and Felix. Our announcer was Gary Owens.

Conflict was ever-present, as these characters lives were truly centered around The Bumble Cable Company, which was what seemingly was being advertised. Here are three of these commercials.

#1 "STAFF MEETING"

SFX: HUB BUB

BUMBLY: Alright. Alright. The regular staff meeting of Bumbly Cable will now come to order.

SFX: GAVEL TAPS

BUMBLY: First order of business. New business. Miss Potter?

POTTER: What?

BUMBLY: Any new business?

POTTER AND FELIX BOTH LAUGH

SFX: GAVEL TAPS

BUMBLY: Decorum people. Alright. Let's move on to old business. Miss Potter?

POTTER: What?

BUMBLY: What about old business?

FELIX: Oh, it's all going to Cross Country Wireless.

SFX: GAVEL POUNDING

BUMBLY: Felix, you're out of order!

FELIX: Oh darn.

BUMBLY: Well, Miss Potter, why?

POTTER: I don't know. Ask him.

BUMBLY: Him?

ANNCR: Hello, I'm the Cross Country Wireless announcer.

BUMBLY: You are?

ANNCR: Yes. Lower rates is why everyone's going to Cross Country Wireless.

BUMBLY: How low?

ANNCR: How's free installation and our regular low rate of just $19.95 a month for basic service?

ALL: (In unison) Yikes!

ANNCR: And that includes a converter, remote control and monthly guide and now even the Disney channel.

FELIX: Ooh Disney.

ANNCR: So why bumble around? Call Cross Country Wire. . . .

SFX: GAVEL POUNDING CUTS ANNCR OFF

BUMBLY: Alright, you're out of order! Sergeant at Arms remove that announcer.

POTTER: Mr. Bumbly, we don't have a Sergeant at Arms.

BUMBLY: Alright, Felix, *you're* the Sergeant at Arms.

FELIX: Oh, not me Uncle Bumbly.

BUMBLY: You Miss Potter?

POTTER: I don't think so.

ANNCR: Don't bumble around. Call Cross Country Wireless. 909- 697-5800. That's 909-697-5800.

#2 "ASPIRIN"

BUMBLY: Miss Potter? Felix?

POTTER: What?

BUMBLY: What's going on *now* at Cross Country Wireless?

POTTER: Now they've added Fox Sports West 2 with their basic service.

BUMBLY: What's that?

FELIX: (Enthusiastic) Fox Sports West 2 is a new sports channel, Uncle Bumbly.

BUMBLY: Bid deal. Bumbly Cable has the Bumbly-Mumble-Pegs sports channel.

POTTER: (Sarcastic) Yeah. "All mumble pegs all the time."

FELIX: Fox Sports West 2 on Cross Country has Dodgers home games.

BUMBLY: Dodgers home games?

FELIX: Yeah. And Clippers, Anaheim Mighty Ducks. Even USC and UCLA football and basketball.

BUMBLY: Well there's lots of people who'd much rather watch mumble pegs.

FELIX: (Goofy laugh) Name one, uncle Bumbly.

BUMBLY: Mrs. Bumbly.

POTTER: Yikes.

ANNCR: Don't bumble around. Call Cross Country Wireless. Basic service now includes Fox Sports West 2, just $21.95 a month. And that also includes a remote control and monthly guide. Add two premium channels like HBO, Cinemax or Showtime and installation is free.

BUMBLY: Free? Miss Potter, don't we give our customers something free?

POTTER: Yeah. Free aspirin.

BUMBLY: Aspirin?

FELIX: We include it with their Bumbly Cable bill.

BUMBLY: Miss Potter, shouldn't we charge for that aspirin?

POTTER: Yikes.

ANNCR: Call Cross Country Wireless. 909-697-5800. That's 909-697-5800.

#3 "LET ME LOOK THAT UP"

SFX: PHONE RING/ PICK UP

FELIX: Hello. Bumbly Cable. Okay.

BUMBLY: (Secretive and urgent) Felix, who is it?

FELIX: Oh, a lady uncle Bumbly. Wants to sign up with Bumbly Cable.

BUMBLY: Gimme that phone. (Unctuous) Hello maam, can I help you? What do we charge for basic service? Let me look that up. (Aside.) Miss Potter, how much for basic service?

POTTER: (Matter of factly) A hundred dollars.

BUMBLY: (Back on phone) A hundred dollars, maam. Oh, let me look that up. (Aside. Almost desperate) Miss Potter, is that for a year?

POTTER: No, for a month.

BUMBLY: (Back on phone.) That's for a month maam. Uh, let me look that up. (Aside.) Miss Potter, how much for installation?

POTTER: Well if Felix goes out and does it. . . .

FELIX: Oh goody.

POTTER: We pay them.

BUMBLY: We do?

ANNCR: Don't bumble around. Call Cross Country Wireless. Now get basic service plus HBO, Cinemax and Showtime. Just $29.95 a month for the first three months. And installation is free.

BUMBLY: (On the phone.) Uh you didn't hear that did you maam? Uh, you did?

ANNCR: So call Cross Country Wireless.

BUMBLY: (On phone.) Uh what's that? The Cross Country Wireless phone number? Uh let me look that up.

ANNCR: Call 909-697-5800.

BUMBLY: You know, I don't think they have a number, maam.

ANNCR: Oh yeah? That's 909-697-5800. Cross Country Wireless.

ALL: (In unison) Yikes.

If made well, a radio commercial should be one that listeners will enjoy hearing many times over. With respect to this, it's not uncommon for radio stations to get phone calls from listeners requesting a favorite commercial of theirs. When listeners call radio stations and request a certain commercial, then the advertiser should know that there's some very good radio advertising working for them.

This leads to the question, "Does the time ever come when people get tired of a commercial?" Of course. No commercial is impervious to listening fatigue. However, one that's creatively written and produced is the radio commercial that stands the best chance of holding up to repetition. Oddly, it is sometimes the advertiser who becomes antsy and bored with the commercial. At the advertiser's restless behest, a perfectly fine commercial is sometimes prematurely taken off the air and replaced with something else. This can happen when the commercial is just starting to take hold and make an impact on the listeners.

Commercials are like ingredients that are tossed into a pot. They need to cook and simmer for a while before listeners really get a good whiff of the stew. Advertisers should refrain from pulling a commercial too soon, especially if it's a good one. The life span of a radio commercial is related to its frequency of play. The more a commercial is played and the longer that frequency continues, the more prone it will be to over-staying its welcome.

To avoid this risk, it is wise to include and rotate more than one commercial in a radio buy scheduled to run for more than a few weeks. When the buy is of considerable frequency, then it's even more advisable to run at least two or three different commercials during the schedule. Conversely, a great radio commercial can be rendered totally ineffective and be of no value to the advertiser, if it's not supported with the frequency of a decent media schedule.

Now to the question "For it to be a good, creative radio commercial must it necessarily be humorous?" No. A good, creative radio commercial can be dramatic, poignant, interesting or enlightening.

Some of the finest and most effective commercials are PSA's (Public Service Announcements) that deal with serious subjects like HIV testing, smoking, drug addiction, teen pregnancy, teen violence and spousal and child abuse. Few if any of these commercials are humorous, nor would humor be especially appropriate. When an advertiser truly has something meaningful to say in the commercial, then the creative structure of the message is not nearly as challenging as it would be if the advertiser had little to communicate.

I remember getting a phone call from an advertising agency about doing some radio commercials for a car dealer client of theirs. The call was from the account executive who said that their client wanted to do some very wacky and zany radio spots. This kind of input usually suggests that neither the client or the agency has any sense of advertising or marketing focus. I asked him what it was that their client wanted to communicate about their car dealership in the commercials. He just giggled and said, "Oh, nothing really. They don't care, just as long as the commercials are wacky and zany."

When a client, like this car dealer, wants to advertise on the radio for no other reason than to be wacky and zany, then they would be well advised if their agency account executive reminded them that they are in the business of selling cars, not selling comedy. I disqualified myself from this assignment when the account executive asked me to overnight them a sample tape of some of my wackiest and zaniest radio commercials. I told him that I didn't have any, which was true.

As was suggested earlier, humor in an advertiser's radio commercials can be effective in two respects: enticing and compelling the listener to listen, and casting the advertiser in a positive and favorable light. From a simple advertising perspective, the text of any radio commercial should have more product relevance than merely sixty seconds of people throwing pies into each other's faces.

Being funny just for the sake of being funny is not the creative exercise. Being funny is only valid when it's for the positive sake of the product.

Chapter 11

When Looking for a Forest Can Mean Missing a Tree

It is routine practice at advertising agencies that, once written, a radio commercial script is subject to review and critique by the writer's creative superiors and then by the client. Often, the writer will be required to make revisions in the text of the commercial. This is necessary when there is an inaccuracy or something of a legal nature needs to be included or excluded from the text. Often, there are last-minute copy changes, and sometimes the writer may be asked to rework the creative concept.

When a concept isn't working in the first place, and doesn't seem to be doing any better in the second or third place, then the horse is probably dead and there's no point in whipping it anymore. It's best to let go of what was probably a lousy idea and explore another creative direction.

Several years ago, I was hired by an agency to direct one of their agency-written commercials. A contingent of people flew to Los Angeles the afternoon of the recording session: the agency creative director, the agency producer and two account people. Oddly, neither the writer nor a client representative, like the marketing or advertising director, made the trip. I thought this odd, because the words "Revision #7. Approved for production," were written at the top of the script.

Revision number 7? To this day, I sometimes bolt up in the middle of the night out of a fretful sleep and wonder "what could have possibly been wrong with revision number 6?"

A script with so many revisions could only mean that the client had obviously played a very active, if not obsessive, role in the creative evolution of this radio commercial. The agency people told me that the client had planned to come down and be at the recording session but there had been a last-minute corporate crisis and he was unable to make the trip. With considerable angst, he told the agency people that he would just have to trust all of us to do a good job without him. I, for one, was certain that we could.

As far as everyday radio commercials come and go, this particular one seemed to be fairly ordinary and not especially inspired. It was kind of amazing to me what all this revision fuss was all about.

The creative director told me that the copywriter was a bright, young woman who was new to the agency and was one for whom the agency had high creative expectations. She was also new to radio, and this script that I was about to produce was the very first radio commercial she had ever written. I couldn't help wonder why she wasn't here at the session. It certainly would have been an excellent experience for her to witness and be involved in the production of her radio commercial, but they left her home.

When I'm directing agency-written radio commercials, usually someone will ask if I have any creative suggestions for the script. Most of the time I do, but any ideas I may have pop up as we're recording the voice talent. That's when you can tell if the scripted words are working and the intended humor is playing or not.

I have found that during recording sessions, when the commercial doesn't seem to be working, invariably someone who's in charge, or even someone who thinks they should be in charge, will start directing the talent with a variety of futile instructions. "What if you change your character?" "Try giving it a broader delivery." "Can you make your voice go higher?" "How 'bout you do it with a German accent?" "Now try a French accent." "See if you can make the character more cartooney." "Tell you what, try switching parts." The problem here is not necessarily with how the talent is reading the script but usually with the script. Logically, the way to correct the problem is to doctor the script right there on the spot at the recording session. Obviously, what is needed then is someone there with the authority to say, "Yes, let's do that." Such a person is seldom there. Those there, however, are any number of people who would remind you that the script has already been client-approved and, therefore, any changes are out of the question. To take such a position is to put one's self in a state of creative denial, thereby limiting the commercial's potential effectiveness. Of course, if the commercial is devoid of any potential effectiveness, then any play-doctoring would mean starting from scratch and writing another commercial.

As far as the commercial at hand was concerned, it was apparent that the agency people were not looking for me to come up with revision number 8. I strongly sensed that I should just do what they hired me to do and leave it at that.

Beside the issue of whether the humor is working or not, it is important that the writer always has a clear and detailed picture of the scene in their mind before committing that scene to paper. If the writer hasn't clearly visualized what they are writing, then what the listener hears will be visually vague and confusing. An example of this was apparent in a brief scene in the middle of the commercial. The scene was only about three seconds long and it was the first thing that we recorded.

SFX: Traffic Jam. Gridlock. Horns honking

MAN: (Irate. From his car.) Hey pal, you're in the wrong lane!

We recorded the man's voice track "wild," or separately, from the rest of the commercial. His voice track would then be mixed into the rest of the commercial later, with the sound effects of honking horns and traffic jam ambiance. In the studio, I asked the actor to deliver the line in a series of five different "takes" with varying degrees of intensity and irritation. Each of his readings was fine and exactly to our projected time.

I then went into the control booth where all were happily in accord that "take" number four was their choice. I wouldn't have had any problem if they had selected take number one, two, three or five.

Their focus was strictly on how the actor's line sounded, but my focus was on what the line meant. I was having trouble with how "Hey pal, you're in the wrong lane," connected to the clarity and staging of this scene in the listener's mind.

I tried to "take a picture" in my own mind, but nothing seemed to develop. Where, I asked myself, is the guy in the wrong lane? Better yet, which lane is the wrong lane and where is this in relation to our guy in his car shouting "Hey pal, you're in the wrong lane?" I was stymied.

If the writer did have a clear picture of this scene, then about the only thing I could imagine was another car facing in the same direction to our guy's immediate left. That would put the guy in a lane where traffic was coming directly towards him, which meant that a head-on collision was momentarily imminent. If that was how the writer pictured this scene, then by the time the listener would have figured out where the guy in the wrong lane was, the commercial would be over.

My hunch is that the writer really didn't consider any staging details for this scene, other than it was just three seconds of an average traffic jam, and the line, "Hey pal, you're in the wrong lane," seemed to be a generically appropriate thing to say.

Admittedly, I was focusing on a small detail, but the last thing audio cues should do is distract from the progression of the commercial by confusing the listener. With all of the nit-picking this script had been subjected to, nobody picked up on the incongruity of this simple, little moment. When I called attention to it, I immediately became the recipient of multiple raised eyebrows and some testy stares. "Well" one of the raised eyebrows said, "what would you suggest that the guy say?" Now I had to slip on my diplomacy hat. "Well, I'm certainly not opting for another script revision. Heaven knows, you've gone through more than your share of those. But, all seriousness aside, and with all due respect to your new, very creative, yet fledgling radio writer, I would simply have the guy lean on his horn and then yell out 'Hey pal, move it!' But what the heck, a traffic jam is a traffic jam and if everybody's happy with 'Hey pal, you're in the wrong lane,' then let's press on."

They all looked at each other for a long moment, then the creative director turned to the actor, who had casually wandered into the control room and said, "Would you mind going back into the studio and giving us the line, 'Hey pal, move it?' You know, just like you did with 'Hey pal, you're in the wrong lane.' "

I was glad to see that someone with the authority to make an on-the-spot decision like that was at this recording session.

Chapter 12

When You've Just Made the World's Funniest Radio Commercial

Cliff Einstein is one of the founders of Dailey & Associates Advertising in Los Angeles, and he is also the creative director and the CEO. I have known and worked with Cliff and his agency on several occasions over the years.

One Friday, during the late 70s at about eleven o'clock in the morning, I got a call from Cliff. I always enjoyed hearing from him because I find him very amusing. This was the gist of the phone call:

CLIFF: Barz?

BARZ: Cliff?

CLIFF: How's it goin' Barz?

BARZ: Good Cliff. How 'bout you?

CLIFF: Barz, what are you doing today?

BARZ: Me? I don't know, nothing much.

CLIFF: See, we have this wine account, Guild wine. They're up in San Francisco.

BARZ: Ok.

CLIFF: One of their wines is this brand called Vino Da Tavola.

BARZ: Uhuh.

CLIFF: That's Italian for "Wine of the table" Barz.

BARZ: So it is.

CLIFF: It's a pretty cheap wine.

BARZ: Uhuh.

CLIFF: Not exactly a premium wine.

BARZ: Right.

CLIFF: See, we gotta do a radio spot for them.

BARZ: Uhuh.

CLIFF: Dick Popson, our account guy, has to present something to them in San Francisco Monday morning.

BARZ: Today's Friday, Cliff.

CLIFF: Right. What if Popson and I come over to your place, say in about an hour and we'll bring a couple bottles of the wine, you know, in lieu of money.

BARZ: Wine in lieu of money?

CLIFF: Yeah, we don't really have much of a budget for this. See we can drink the wine while we write a funny radio spot. It'll be sort of like a party.

BARZ: Uhuh. So what'll Popson do?

CLIFF: Oh, he'll watch us.

BARZ: Uhuh. Ok, but bring the wine in a brown paper bag.

Well about an hour later, in my office, we were working on a radio script, as well as working on the wine. "So what do we say about this wine?" I asked. "Well, we really can't talk about how socially elevating it is," Cliff pointed out. "So should we allude to the fact that it's cheap?" I asked. "Inexpensive," Cliff said.

Since people were not terribly familiar with this brand, we thought it was important to call attention to the red checkered tablecloth label on the Vino da Tavola bottle "So if people heard our commercial, then they'd recognize the wine when they saw it in the markets," Cliff said. "Uhuh," I concurred.

Now for the concept: An inept, ostensibly continental wine-taster, who can't tell one wine from another, is wrongly trying to identify a wine, then proudly identifies Vino da Tavola because he peeked at the label. Immediately, Arte Johnson of the then popular TV show *Laugh In* came to mind. He would be the perfect character for our wine-taster.

When writing humor for a specific character, it is helpful to have a specific voice talent in mind. A familiarity with the available pool of voice talent, and the range of their characterizations and voice qualities, makes this possible. It's better to tailor and custom fit a suit for a specific person's measurements than to make the suit and hope to find someone who will fit into it. That's one reason why I have never been thrilled with the process of auditioning. But more on the subject of voice auditions and casting later.

By five o'clock that afternoon, Cliff and I had a sixty second commercial scripted, and we were convinced that we had just written the world's funniest radio commercial. Of course, the wine we had been liberally sampling as we went along may have had something to do with our creative euphoria. The wine wasn't really too bad once we got past the first bottle.

Nonetheless, we all agreed that Dick Popson should not go up to San Francisco Monday and merely present this script. What we should do is record and produce an air-ready demo and arm Popson with that to present to the Vino da Tavola client.

"But wait a minute," I said, "when are we going to record this?" "How 'bout tonight?" Cliff said. To which I replied, "Fine, but it's Friday night." Cliff said, "So? Let's see if we can get a recording studio." "Fine," I said again and called a studio. "Ok we're booked at eight o'clock tonight at Bell Sound."

Things were falling into place. Now only one slight detail remained: Who do we get at this late hour on a Friday night to do the voices? So Cliff says, "How 'bout Arte Johnson as the the wine-taster, Barz, you as the guy and Tom Bosley as the announcer?" "Excellent cast," I said, "Getting Barz is no problem, but Arte Johnson and Tom Bosley, I don't know." Then Cliff says, "Why don't you call their agents and see if we can book them?"

Because we were well into the dinner hour, and their agents were probably long gone and well into their weekend, I simply called Arte and Tom at their respective homes. "Sorry to be calling with this last-minute notice," I said, "but I'm asking you to voice a radio demo tonight in the name of creative brilliance."

Arte and Tom each told me that as much as they appreciate creative brilliance, and would really love to do it, they each had other plans. "I understand completely," I said. Then I proceeded to beg and grovel "Pleeaase, oh pleeaase, someday I'll write all about this in a book and I'll even mention how wonderful and talented you are. Oh, pleeaase do this demo, or I'll see to it that you never work again in this town."

Either out of pity or fear, Arte and Tom each graciously reconsidered and canceled their respective previous engagements. Like the real troopers that they are, they were at the recording studio promptly at eight p.m.

Suddenly, two hours had flown by, and our brilliant demo was finished and ready for Dick Popson to take to San Francisco and play for the client Monday morning. The entire process, from creative concept to completed production, took exactly nine hours and two bottles of wine. Here is the commercial.

SFX: Wine bottle cork pop. Wine pour.

BOSLEY: Here now is the wine-taster.

SFX: Sipping

ARTE: (quirky accent) This is a Chateau de Nouf de Pape . . . 1956.

BARZ: No.

ARTE: Mm-huh. It is a red burgundy, very old, very fruitful. A very nice bouquet. A Margaux from the Loire. 49, no?

BARZ: No.

ARTE: A white burgundy, perhaps very recent from Spain.

BARZ: Wrong.

ARTE: Champagne?

BARZ: No.

ARTE: Beer?

BARZ: No.

ARTE: Root Beer.

BARZ: Never mind.

ARTE: Hot chocolate.

SFX: Wine pour

BARZ: Here try this.

SFX: Sipping

ARTE: Ah. Vino da Tavola!

BARZ: That's right.

ARTE: Ah-hah. One in a row!

BOSLEY: Vino da Tavola. The great inexpensive table wine with the red checkered tablecloth on the label.

BARZ: Uh, how did you know it was Vino da Tavola?

ARTE: I saw the red checkered napkin on the label.

BARZ: Wrong.

ARTE: The red napkin on the checkered tablecloth?

BARZ: No.

ARTE: Can you give me a hint?

BOSLEY: Guild Wine Company. Lodi, California.

There are two points about the business of creating, producing and presenting a humorous radio commercial to the client that are worth mentioning. First, in terms of turn around time, a radio commercial can be written, cast, recorded and produced quite quickly. While nine hours and two bottles of wine is nothing to sneeze at, I'm sure that in a real pinch a few hours could even be shaved off of that, with or without the wine.

The second thing is that creative people should never get their creative hopes up too high. No matter how creatively terrific they think they've done, they shouldn't be surprised if the client thinks otherwise.

Here is the resolution of this brief wine commercial saga.

(The following Monday, about noon, Cliff calls.)

CLIFF: Barz?

BARZ: Cliff?

CLIFF: Popson just called from San Francisco.

BARZ: So, how did it go?

CLIFF: You know the Golden Gate Bridge?

BARZ: Sure, lovely bridge.

CLIFF: Well Popson's gonna jump from it.

BARZ: Oh, so the client didn't like the spot, hunh?

CLIFF: Barz, the client didn't think it was funny.

BARZ: You know what Cliff?

CLIFF: What?

BARZ: When the client doesn't think it's funny. . . .

CLIFF: I know. . . .

BOTH: (Together). . . it's not funny.

CLIFF: So what'll we do, try coming up with something else?

BARZ: I think you're already over budget.

CLIFF: Oh, right.

BARZ: In the meantime, though, I would try to contact the bridge.

CLIFF: Yeah, I should tell Popson not to jump.

Something very important that I taught myself long ago is when the client doesn't think that the commercial is funny, it is only an exercise in futility to try to convince the client otherwise. Therefore, the commercial is not funny.

Needless to say, Vino da Tavola didn't end up with a radio commercial. A short time later, I got another call from Cliff.

CLIFF: Barz?

BARZ: Cliff?

CLIFF: Guess what?

BARZ: What?

CLIFF: Looks like they dropped the brand.

BARZ: You mean Vino da Tavola's gone?

CLIFF: Uhuh, and so is the marketing guy Popson presented our radio commercial to.

BARZ: Hmm. No wonder he didn't think it was funny.

Chapter 13

Clang, Bam, Crash, Boing, Clunk and Silence

Sound effects are what make radio commercials tick, explode, howl, growl and go bump in the night. They are the elements that set the scene: rushing water, running footsteps, crickets chirping, dogs barking, screeching cat, galloping horse, snarling lion, telephone ringing.

How and where a sound effect is placed in the commercial is critical to what the listener will visualize. A sound effect is like a radio commercial's camera. It can be used to pan by a thundering herd of elephants, truck along side of a jogging marathon runner, or zoom in on a mosquito. Sound effects can fade, cross fade, dissolve and even be cut and edited.

Specific sound effects, with background ambiance, set and place the scene and assist in moving the characters about in a given environment. A sound effect can even work the same way that a prop or gesture does to punctuate or accent the humor: the proverbial rim-shot after a punch line or the "thwack" of flesh hitting the water when the diver does a belly flop.

Sound effects were running gags in some of radio's favorite old comedy shows, like *Fibber McGee and Molly*. Hardly an episode went by when Fibber McGee wouldn't tell Molly that he was going to get something out of the closet and Molly would shriek "Don't open that closet!" Of course he would, and once opened there was always a slight moment of silence. This slight moment of silence was the predictable lull before the storm so to speak. And the lull was the audience's signal to break into laughter in anticipation of the sound effect tumult of stuff and junk that invariably came tumbling and crashing down moments after Fibber McGee opened the closet.

In *The Jack Benny Program,* an obsessively frugal Jack Benny would periodically decide to visit his money. His money was secured and kept in a subterranean vault many leagues under his house. Jack Benny's trip down to this vault was in itself a sound effects trip. This was punctuated by a hilarious cacophony of metallic sounds of locks, latches and steel gates clanking open then shut, coupled with Jack Benny's seemingly endless echoed footsteps as he walked down and deeper down to the vault. Once there, he would be greeted by Ed (Mel Blanc), his lonely and socially isolated vault guard. Forlornly, Ed would ask about the outside world like, "Is World War II over yet?"

The idea of Jack Benny visiting his money in his subterranean vault was certainly funny in itself, but it was the placement and the timing of those wonderful sound effects that made the scene even funnier.

Jack Benny also had a jalopy of a car—an old, dilapidated Maxwell. Everyone who ever listened to his show had a very distinct picture of Jack Benny's old Maxwell in their mind. This image was vividly painted when Rochester, his all around man servant, butler, confidant and chauffeur, would get behind the wheel and attempt to start the antiquated and broken down motor.

Through a succession of outrageous sounds, the Maxwell sputtered, coughed, wheezed, gasped, burped, back fired and finally chugged, all to the roar and delight of the studio audience. Many of these sounds were created vocally by the brilliant and versatile Mel Blanc.

Little else in a radio commercial helps jump start the listener's imagination than a good sound effect. If an effect is not immediately recognizable, however, then it can only serve to confuse the listener. When writing unusual, or offbeat sound effects into a commercial, the writer should always consider flagging the effect by first referencing it in the spoken text before it is heard.

Of course, most sound effects commonly used in radio commercials are immediately recognizable to the ear: phone ringing, door bell or door knock, door opening and closing, car starting and driving off. These and many other sounds speak for themselves, however, some don't.

Recently, I saw a radio script that began like this:

SFX: Shower Sounds

MAN: (Singing in Shower)

The problem here is that the writer obviously knows that the singing man is in the shower, but will it be perfectly clear to the listener? Or, will the listener merely wonder what that odd "shhssing" sound is?

Sometimes an inexperienced radio writer will put a sound effect into a script and assume that because it's indicated in the script, then automatically everyone will know what the sound effect is. Listeners never see the script, they only hear the commercial.

What needs to happen with our fellow singing in the shower is to establish right away where he is: in a shower. A few seconds need to be allocated at the beginning of the commercial to accommodate this reference, e.g.:

SFX: Shower Curtain Pull

MAN: (Mutters) Ah. Now for a nice, hot shower.

SFX: Shower Faucet Knob Turn On. Shower Sounds

MAN: (Begins to sing)

Let's say that the writer has created a scene in a commercial where a volcano erupts. To find this sound effect, the producer and the sound engineer would probably have to review any number of explosion "cuts" from the studio's sound-effects library. As a matter of fact, the exact sound of a volcano erupting may even exist in the sound effects library. But just because it says "volcano eruption" in the library's catalog doesn't necessarily mean that the listener will hear this volcano in the radio commercial as anything other than some kind of explosion. In any event, the listener should be alerted to the fact that the forthcoming "explosion" is indeed a volcano erupting, e.g.:

LADY: I say Charles, what do you suppose that large plume of smoke suddenly billowing from the top of that mountain means?

MAN: Well, if you ask me Denise, I'd say that mountain is an active volcano, and it looks like it's about to erupt.

LADY: Erupt? You don't say.

MAN: I do say.

SFX: Kablaam! (Volcano Erupts.)

Of course, many unusual and strange sound effects often require some engineering ingenuity and innovation, like combining and mixing together several various sounds.

I once had to create the sound of a male walrus' mating call. Neither I nor the sound engineer I was working with had ever been in the company of a walrus in the throes of calling for a mate, so we pretty much had to wing it when trying to replicate it's amorous wail. I believe that we ended up combining a cow mooing with a barking seal and then for good measure we added a donkey braying. We smoothed it all out in the mix with a little reverb.

What we ended up with could have easily been mistaken as the sound of a sick jack ass or even a deranged moose. This really wasn't a problem, because the script had already established that this woeful cry that was about to be heard was indeed the call of a sexually aroused walrus.

All professional recording studios, especially the ones geared to the recording and production of commercials, have extensive sound effects libraries as well as licensed "needle drop" music libraries.

There are times when I like, and even prefer, to tinker around with certain "hand made" sound effects. This requires a little patience and some trial and error. Sometimes, an appropriate or even a unique sound effect can be made with various items and utensils found laying around the house or even the recording studio. I've found that when humorous or fanciful cranking, ratchet or squeaking sounds are needed, merely winding or cranking up and recording little toys can often perfectly fill a sound effects bill.

I have a voice actor friend, Frank Welker. Frank is well known in the business, especially for his wonderful and varied cartoon voices. Frank is also a human sound-effects machine because he can do an amazing number of vocal sound effects. Just tell him what you want, and the sound effect will come gyrating out of his mouth. I'm not sure which is funnier, the sound effect he produces, or watching him trying to produce it.

His barking dogs are especially impressive. On many occasions I have opted to hire Frank to growl, bark or yelp in a radio commercial, rather than having to rely on finding appropriate "canned" dog barks in a sound-effects library. Besides, Frank Welker's live barking dogs are much funnier than the prerecorded real ones. The other remarkable thing about his barking dogs effects is that he can do just about any kind: anything from the sound of a yipping, little Llahsa Apso to a deep, full-throated "wahooff" of a Great Dane. His cat meows and screeches, horse whinnies, lion snarls and roars, croaking frogs and even his crickets are equally as amazing as they are amusing.

The other two elements that the writer of radio commercials has at their disposal are silence and music. Silence, as we were all once taught, is or should be golden, and so it can be in the text of a humorous radio commercial. Whether it's a slight pregnant pause or a few beats of nothing, silence is often the perfect timing touch that makes the humor play.

For the most part, however, silence is seldom used as a production element in radio commercials for the simple reason that there's seldom any time for it. Furthermore, during that brief moment of silence, a radio station could interpret that dead air as the end of the commercial and cut the commercial off the air. So my rule about silence in radio commercials is to be careful of how you use it.

Old time radio shows were a treasure chest filled with wonderful examples of the humorous timing effects of silence. One of the classic uses was once again, on *The Jack Benny Program.*

In one of the episodes, Jack Benny is walking down the street and a thug comes up behind him and says, "Your money or your life." There is silence. The thug repeats, "Your money or your life." There is more silence. By now the thug is exasperated, "I said, your money or your life!" To which Jack Benny nonchalantly replies, "I'm thinking about it."

Chapter 14

Music and Jingles: The Artificial Sweeteners

When one thinks of music in radio advertising, the first thing that comes to mind is jingles. Jingles are as old as radio commercials themselves. So what exactly is a jingle? Simply, it's an advertiser's slogan put to music with usually a few more words added to it. A jingle can glorify a product by musically lifting it to heights never before imagined by the folks in product development, brand management or marketing.

Although a vacuum cleaner is merely a household appliance that sucks up dirt from the carpet, a lush jingle can make it the catalyst for loving families happily gathering together at the holidays and the reason why the children grew up and all became plastic surgeons.

A jingle can even serve to work inspirational, internal wonders for the advertiser. It can reinforce the corporate notion, especially with the people in upper management, that what they manufacture and sell is indeed a glorious and incredible thing.

However, jingles certainly aren't the only way that music is utilized in radio commercials. Music can also be used as a production element for dramatic emphasis or to score a commercial. Music is also used as a background or ambient element, most often to underscore a one-voice monologue commercial. Music is often used as the product's identifying theme. Unlike a jingle, theme music is instrumental. Most theme music in commercials, especially for the larger national advertisers, are original compositions.

The least expensive and most common way to use instrumental music in radio commercials is with licensed and prerecorded music track cuts from one of many "needle drop" music libraries. Access to music libraries is usually found at most recording studios. A nominal fee is paid to the licenser for each "needle drop" music cut that's used in a given commercial. Using production music in this manner is considerably less expensive than original music. Brief music cuts like fanfares, musical billboards, intros, extros, bridges and stings are also used as embellishments, accents or dramatic punctuations. Many of these kinds of music elements are often also found in a recording studio's sound effects library.

Music was common in old radio shows, especially organ intros, bridges and extros in soap operas like, *Portia Faces Life* and game shows like *The Quiz Kids,* while dramatic and scary musical flourishes were common in mystery shows like *The Shadow, Inner Sanctum* and *I Love a Mystery.* It's hard to find any old radio program where music didn't play a role in its overall identity and sound. Of course, when it came to commercials there was hardly a cereal, cigarette, toothpaste, soap or coffee that didn't have it's own jingle musical identity or musical theme.

Some of the music heard in commercials today has been adapted from popular hit songs or classic compositions. Unless in public domain, the rights to this music for adaptation to commercials must be acquired from the publishers of the music. When obtaining the rights of a deceased composer's work, negotiations may also be necessary with that composer's estate.

The precedence for advertisers acquiring and then adapting the music of well known composers to their commercials probably goes back to the early days of radio. When hearing a performance of Ferde Grofe's "Grand Canyon Suite", radio listeners were likely to recognize it as the theme music for Philip Morris cigarettes. Similarly today, when people hear the great American classic, "Rhapsody in Blue," they are probably reminded of the United Airlines commercials. In either case, I don't think that Grofe or Gershwin had theme music for commercials in mind when they composed their music.

Today, large sums of money can be put into the development and production of a jingle package. This music is then primarily used in television commercials behind the visuals. What usually goes over a jingle in a radio commercial is an announcer or speaking voices.

In order to properly place speaking voices against a jingle, portions of the vocals often need to be mixed out of the jingle track so that what is being spoken is only spoken over instrumental sections of the jingle track. Speaking of "spoken," it is an unspoken rule that voices should never speak on top of singers vocalizing in a jingle.

Another way in which a jingle is used in radio commercials is to edit and remix its conclusive vocal phrase and then tag or end the commercial with it. This is known as a "signature" or "button tag."

When writing such a commercial, it is always important to take into account that this tag element may require 8 or 10 seconds of time, so that needs to be factored into the overall time of the commercial. The function of a jingle tag used in this manner is ostensibly to conclude and bring down the curtain on the commercial. It's underlying purpose, however, is to musically end the commercial with the advertiser's slogan.

I have, at times, been in a studio about to produce a 60 second agency commercial when someone out of the blue casually says, "Oh, by the way, we also have this 10 second jingle tag that we have to put on the end of the commercial." This is said, after having projected split-second timings for voices and sound effects, which would bring this commercial neatly out to 59.9 seconds. So much for split-second timings.

Today, most original jingles, especially the ones for large national advertisers, are designed and orchestrated to reflect a contemporary young and "with it" sound. Whatever style of music that's currently in vogue is the sound advertisers often prefer in their jingles.

Advertisers should not expect to realize any great music identity or awareness benefits from a jingle on radio, unless the jingle is used with considerable frequency over an extensive period of time.

It is never a wise decision to buy a limited number of radio stations with a short-term schedule lacking frequency. To do it with the idea of just running a jingle during that schedule is simply a lot less wise.

I suppose that the reason why I'm not such a big fan of jingles is because you really can't say very much in the context of one. Besides, there's already plenty of music on the radio as it is.

Chapter 15

Producing Radio Commercials: First We'll Need Some Voices

I once spoke on the subject of creating and producing radio commercials at the Advertising Age Creative Workshop in Chicago. Attending my one-hour session were about a hundred advertising agency principals and creative people from around the country, as well as some client advertising managers and marketing directors.

My session was in two parts. For the first half hour, I spoke about creating and writing radio commercials, and the second half hour was devoted to talking about recording and producing them.

Throughout the session, I noticed that everyone seemed to be very preoccupied with the business of taking notes. I thought this was somewhat odd because I was not telling them much that was particularly insightful or noteworthy. Notes of this kind are seldom if ever revisited, and I honestly believe that the reason people take them is because they're afraid that they might forget something of importance that is being said.

When I got to the mid point in the presentation, I said, "Once a radio commercial has been written and then approved, the next thing is to record and produce it."

By no means was this an earth-shattering insight or revelation. To my amazement, all one hundred people in the audience immediately hunched over their note pads and with pencils in hand proceeded to take note of that. I couldn't resist, so I said, "And remember, you heard it here first." And you know what? Quite a few wrote that down too.

There's some kind of relevance to radio listening here, and I think it has to do with preoccupation. In the case of my speech, no one seemed to really be listening because they were so preoccupied with the task of taking notes.

As was suggested earlier, radio listeners too are usually preoccupied attending to other things when listening to the radio. While one of them probably isn't taking notes about what's being said in the commercial, this does seem to corroborate the need to snap listeners out of their preoccupations and entice them into focusing on just listening. Which also suggests that perhaps my workshop presentation could have used some additional "snap."

Let's talk about what happens once the radio scripts have been written and approved for production. The first thing is casting: the business of selecting the voice talent.

So where and how does one find and obtain voice talent? In larger cities, most professional voice talents are represented by a commercial talent agency. It is normally through commercial talent agencies or agents that voice talents are engaged. The two main centers for voice talent are Los Angeles and New York.

The process of casting can be easy and effortless, or it can be cumbersome and laborious. How the casting process goes is contingent upon who is trusting whom to make the voice-selection decisions. These decisions, while critical to the quality and character of the commercial, aren't really that difficult or complex to make.

So what if it's left up to the writer to select the voices? After all, the writer is the one who created the characters that the voices will be doing. Sorry, but agencies, as well as their clients, don't seem to be confident or comfortable leaving these casting decisions up to the writer alone. By the same token, many agency writers don't even want to assume that responsibility.

Ok, then how about an agency broadcast producer? Sorry again, but agency producers seem to be much more adept at arranging for auditions than they are at selecting or casting voices.

So is there anyone involved in the production process, who's qualified, trusted or even willing to step up to the plate and take a swing at choosing some voices? For the most part, no.

What about an outside creative radio production company who may have been engaged by the advertising agency to produce the commercial? Certainly their expertise and experience would give them the credibility and capability to cast the voices, yes? Yes! However, advertising agencies and advertisers are even tentative about trusting these people.

Casting, therefore, has become an extremely big deal. For the most part, it's done in stages initially by a committee of assorted people at the advertising agency. However, the final casting decision is usually deferred to the client advertiser to make. To me, that makes about as much sense as a surgeon showing his patient an array of knives, then asking the patient to choose the one he'd like the surgeon to use on him during the operation.

The reality is, that when it comes to casting, the advertising agencies have little or no idea who's out there in voice land. This, in spite of the fact that most of them have shelves and boxes full of talent agency house and individual voice tapes and CDs on file.

What totally consumes this casting stage of the commercial-making process is auditions. In terms of money, this process can be very time consuming and therefore, quite costly.

On any given day, it is not unusual, especially in Los Angeles and New York, to find scores of voice actors jammed into their talent agency or a casting service reception room waiting their turn to audition. Often it's for a voice in a commercial that may have as few as two or three words to speak.

Casting today has become a serendipitous procedure subject to how many people are in on the process and how much consensus there is regarding the kind of voice or voices they're all looking for.

In the final analysis, committee-casting does not insure that the best or ideal voice will be selected. There is no guarantee whatsoever. More often than not, the voice that is ultimately selected, is little more than a compromise choice.

Dave liked voice #12 and so did Michelle. Lisa and Mr. Kremmelman kind of liked voice #47. Kevin liked voice #6, but Brian and Debby thought voice #6 sounded too old. Mr. Kremmelman also liked voice #31, but no one else did. However, more peoples' third choice was voice #47, which beat out some of the others' second choice, which was voice #9. But everybody's fourth choice seemed to be voice #3, which was nobody's favorite or second or even third favorite, but what the heck, nobody really hated it either. So voice #3 is the committee's choice.

As a rule, auditioning is either done through talent agencies or casting services. I might interject that the word casting is somewhat of a misnomer. Casting services do not cast the voices; they audition them. I have been lobbying to have that changed to "audition services," but it looks like I'm being stonewalled on this.

The differences between arranging for auditions through talent agencies or casting services are basically as follows:

A talent agency has a number, or "stable," of voice actors that it represents. When a talent agency is asked by an advertising agency to provide them with auditions for a commercial, the talent agency will call a certain number of voice talents (their clients) to read for that audition.

Often, the advertising agency might request to hear specific voice talents who are represented by that talent agency. Talent agencies do not charge for these audition services. It is their hope that one or more of the people that they represent will be cast for the job and in turn they will be compensated by receiving a commission (10%) on the talent fee.

Casting services, on the other hand, do not receive commissions on talent fees and they can draw upon a much more extensive pool of voice people that they choose to audition. This is because they normally will call a wider range of voice talents from several different talent agencies. Unlike talent agency auditioning services that are free, casting companies charge a fee to the advertising agency for providing these audition services.

Whether auditions are done at the offices of a talent agency or at a casting service, they are always recorded. Cassette tapes or CDs of these auditions are then dispatched to the advertising agency. Unless it's otherwise urgent, these audition tapes are likely to sit on someone's desk at the advertising agency for several days or weeks until all of the members of the casting committee can be rounded up and assembled to review these auditions and begin the task of picking a voice. The selected voice, at this stage, is really the agency's recommended voice. Sometimes the recommendation might even include several "finalist" voices. It is then the client advertiser who ultimately will choose and approve the voice.

It should be mentioned that there are instances when, after the auditions have been completed, the whole process turns out to be for naught. This can capriciously happen when the client advertiser has a sudden change of mind and the decision is made to not produce the commercial.

There are also times when a less than straight-forward advertising agency will use the auditioning process simply as a ruse for the purpose of plucking out a professional voice from the audition tapes. The agency would then use the voice in a new creative presentation they are preparing to make to an existing client or to a potential new client. This, of course, is highly irregular and terribly unfair to the voice talent, as well as the talent agency.

Either of these scenarios can provide a clue to a question that voice talents often ask, "Who was it who got booked on that commercial we just auditioned for?" The answer, of course, is "Nobody."

Chapter 16

Doing Voice Work: To Aspire or Not to Aspire

Let's look at the business of voicing commercials. Whether it is radio or television or both, voicing commercials really is a business and it's an extremely competitive one.

While many working and successful voice people, on the advice of their accountants, have turned themselves into corporate entities, it's not likely that you'll find any of these corporations listed in Fortune's 500.

Has anyone ever told you that you've got a nice voice and that you ought to be doing radio and television commercials? Has that same anyone suggested that there's no reason why you couldn't easily be making lots of money doing voice work? Has it ever crossed your mind about giving it a try and putting yourself out there and going after voice work in commercials in earnest? Well, if you do decide to do it, do yourself a large favor: Don't give up your day job. At least, not right away.

In this chapter, I'll try to give the considering voice person some frank and pragmatic reasons to either continue or discontinue considering.

Unlike the effort, time and commitment it takes to acquire a special skill, like learning how to play the harp or juggling several chain saws at one time, if you have a voice, you probably already know how to use it. There isn't a heck of a lot for you to acquire. You can, I suppose, fool around with your voice and with practice learn how to manipulate and make it do other things that it normally wouldn't do.

You could also join a voice workshop, which is somewhat like joining a gym. In this case, what you are working out is your voice. No matter what you do to change or try to turn it into something else, your voice is something that you're pretty much stuck with. So accept, admire and go forward with it as it is. As for the time, effort and commitment that you'll be putting into your voice career, you're likely to find that the time and effort part have more to do with getting voice work than actually doing it.

The first prerequisite to doing voices in commercials is that you must be able to read. That shouldn't be a problem, unless however, someone has been reading this book to you.

Next, you should be able to speak and deliver the words that you are reading and make them come out sounding as if you're not reading them.

This requires that you have some acting skills. You don't have to be a great thespian, but you still have to make those words sound like they're coming from you and not off of a written page. It's also helpful if you can make them sound natural and believable. For a good share of people, this is a relatively easy and effortless thing to do. Of course, if you can't do that, I would suggest that you skip to the next chapter and forget this nonsense about doing voice-overs.

Once you have established that you can speak the written words and indeed make those words sound like they're naturally flowing from your tongue, the next thing to think about is just exactly what your voice does and how many different things you can do with it.

Get to Know Your Voice

This is important because your voice is the product that you and your agent are going to be selling. If neither of you are thoroughly familiar with the nuances of how this product works and what it can or cannot do, then selling it in the competitive voice market place is not going to be easy.

It's really quite amazing that most people haven't got the foggiest notion what their voice actually sounds like, especially to others.

Ask yourself, perhaps with the help of a friend, "what exactly does my voice sound like?" You should listen to and study it. Is it a commanding, rich, resonant voice? Is it a pleasant, generic sounding voice? Is it perhaps nasal or even somewhat abrasive? When you speak, does your voice sound calm and relaxed or does it have a hyper or quick-paced edge to it? Is it a wimpy or nerdy or a timid, mousy little voice? Does it sound young, middle aged, old or ageless? Is it a crackly or scratchy voice? Does it have an accent or regional twang? Is it maybe some of all of the above? Or is it totally something else? Put your voice under the microscope and scrutinize it's quality and sound.

Once you've got a fix on what your voice sounds like, then the next thing to figure out is how many different things you can do with it. How flexible is it? Can you raise it an octave and still speak naturally? Can you make it sound deeper, authoritative, pompous or dignified? Can you make it sound like a spoof of someone authoritative, pompous or dignified? Can you make it sound younger or older? If you do have an accent or twang, can you make it go away? (Probably not, hunh?) If your voice isn't quirky or off beat, can you make it sound that way? Or when you do that does it come out sounding phony or cartooney?

What about characterizations with accents or dialects: British, Irish, French, German, Italian, southern belle or good ole boy, country boy, cowboy, gum-chewing waitress or Bronx cab driver?

If you're not really great at doing characters with accents or dialects *don't* consider including them in your repertoire of voices. There will always be someone who can do them much better or authentically and yours will therefore pale by comparison.

Concentrate and Focus on Defining Your Own Individual Sound

Obviously, the best of all voice over possibilities is for you to discover that your voice genuinely has a truly original, engaging and identifiable quality and sound to it. This is a one of a kind voice. Be it wry, droll, laconic, laid back, tongue-in-cheek or energetically quirky, it's a voice that stands out and can significantly contribute to a commercial's overall concept and character. In addition to television commercial voice overs, people with voices like this, as a rule, make excellent players in dialogue radio commercials.

If you do not have such a voice, be assured that you are not alone in the fraternity of voice-over people because few actually do.

Such a voice can often do well in commercials, but because it's usually so recognizable, this kind of voice does run the risk of being over exposed or identified with a certain product. For the aspiring or beginning voice person, however, being over exposed in voice work should be the least of one's concerns.

After you have gone through this voice self analysis, then you should have a pretty good idea of what your voice is all about.

Get to Know and Understand the Voices Market Place

Watch and listen to lots of commercials. Study them and pay particular attention to the voices and voice overs. Watch television commercials more for spokesperson voices and listen to radio commercials for announcer, spokesperson, dialogue and character voices. Study the commercials in terms of their tonality and consider how you would have delivered the voice-over lines differently.

Familiarize yourself with the delivery styles and character of the voices you hear and evaluate how your voice and style of delivery would fit in and compete for the same kind of voice-over parts. See if you can spot a current proclivity towards using the same types of voices.

Try to get an idea of how many of the commercials are voiced by men as opposed to women. In terms of ratio, you'll probably find that men seem to get significantly more of the spokesperson work.

While advertisers would be vehement in their denial, age discrimination of sorts does exist when it comes to the casting of their spokesperson voices. Younger sounding voices seem to be the advertisers' preference. This is because many advertisers want the voices in their commercials to demographically reflect the age group that their commercials are attempting to reach. In today's advertising marketplace, more commercials seem to be trying to speak to a younger population of consumers. This is based on the notion that if advertisers can get younger, under-thirty consumers to buy their products, they will be buying them for a longer time than older consumers would. What this notion neglects to consider is that the over-fifty consumers have most of the money and are living longer. To accommodate the advertisers' desire to reach a younger market, much of television's current programming is reflected in the spate of edgy dating programs, edgy sitcoms and edgy reality shows, all designed to appeal to the edgy under-thirty audience.

While certainly not all voice and voice-overs should sound like they're thirty or younger, this is something to take into consideration when considering where and how your voice would fit in and compete in today's voices market place, which is increasingly becoming peopled with lots more thirty and under sounding voices.

Geographically Survey the Voices Market Place

Like any market place, the voices market place is where the action is. As was mentioned before, Los Angeles and New York are the two cities where voice work is most abundant. It's also where you will find most of the stiffest competition for this work.

Unfortunately, the supply of voice talent far outstrips the demand for it. There is hardly a shortage of good voice actors, especially in Los Angeles and New York.

However, in just about any other major to medium-sized city, there is probably a reasonable amount of voice work to keep a modest pool of competent voice people working. However, I would guess that few in the pool would actually be making a full-time living doing voice work alone.

As you probably know, voice work is not just limited to radio and television commercials. Among other things, there is occasional work doing narrations and voices for sales, training, educational and industrial films and infomercials. However, little of this kind of voice work can be considered regular or steady.

The Voice Tape

A voice tape is the prescribed, if not the official tool of the trade. Without one, you might as well be a plumber without a wrench or a doctor without a stethoscope. It should either be a cassette or CD or both.

The initial objective of a voice tape should be one-fold. It should help you obtain the second basic thing that's needed, which is commercial representation by a commercial agent. Without representation, getting voice work on your own can be a futile task.

Once the services of a commercial agent have been obtained, that in itself is no assurance that voice work is automatically just around the corner. I recommend that you either keep your present line of work or find another one while you are in the process of waiting for your voice career to bear some fruition.

In the meantime, you can take some measures to help push your voice career along. Doing a mailing piece, in addition to sending out your voice tape to key advertising agency production people, casting services and production companies, is a task you should put some effort into. The best place to get your hands on a good and current mailing list is probably right from your agent.

Is there anything else you can do? What about working the phones? You know, calling and trying to talk to and meet with broadcast producers at advertising agencies, production company people and casting directors? Is that a good thing to do? No!

Sending a card or little reminder note to these people once in a while is perfectly fine but don't call and hustle them. Above all, never pop in on them at their offices unannounced. Leave the one-on-one calling and hustling part up to your agent.

Put Your Money Where Your Mouth Is

Up until now you probably haven't spent much of anything on your budding voice career. Maybe you've just looked upon this voice thing as a lark or something to just goof around with. But if you really feel that you've got the goods, and you're definitely intent on professionally pressing on, then now is the time to get ready to spend some money.

In any business there are start-up costs. The initial expenditure you will face in starting up your voice business is making your voice tape. If you are of a mind not to spend anything in this regard, then you're probably not that serious or secure about pursuing voice work.

What Does It Cost to Make a Voice Tape?

When you make your voice tape, much of the cost depends upon how much recording studio time you incur to prepare your tape. A voice tape is not something that you make and then use forever. It continually evolves and changes. Right from the start you must look upon your first pass at it as a work in progress. I can assure you that the first version of your voice tape will certainly not be your last.

The main objective of your voice tape, at this point, is to help you get a reputable agent. This first version is very important as it should showcase your voice's quality and range.

The focus of your tape should be on what you're most comfortable doing, even if that is doing just one thing. You don't have to feel compelled to put a variety of different voices on your tape. Do that only if you believe that you have different voices that are exceptional.

What Kind of Material Should Go on a Voicetape and How Long Should It Be?

The first thing you'll need to do is gather some material to read and record, which should, of course, be advertising copy. Much of this material can be culled from magazine ads. Copy blocks from magazine ads can adequately serve as announcer or spokesperson words.

Better yet, try to get your hands on some actual radio or television commercial scripts. This is not easy, but it is possible to discreetly get a hold of scripts from recording studios, radio and television stations, advertising agencies, production companies, commercial agents, casting services or voice class workshops.

Once you have secured the materials that you'll be recording, then select and plan to record spokesperson or announcer lines, plus any incidental character voices from the material at hand. It's not a bad idea to get a friend, preferably of the opposite sex, to record a few examples of dialogue with you for inclusion on your tape. The reason that this friend should be of the opposite sex is so that they are not confused with you. They should also be fairly good at doing this sort of thing. I say, "fairly," because you don't want this friend sounding better than you.

Plan to record several things, then be selective and use only those tracks on your voice tape that you feel will highlight and showcase what you do best. For an objective second opinion, you might ask your friend to assist with this selection process. Above all, keep your voice tape short and sweet.

Just remember that those who will be listening to it aren't going to want to listen for very long. It's important that the essence of what your voice is all about comes through, not necessarily loud but certainly clear, in about the first thirty seconds of your tape. By then, whoever is listening should have a pretty good idea what your sound is, or if yours is the voice that they're currently looking for.

Most voice tapes I have heard usually run far too long, and many tend to get repetitive by rambling on with too many examples of the same type of thing. I suggest keeping your voice tape well under two minutes, like maybe a minute and a half. That is unless you've got several different vocal tricks up your cords, then obviously your voice tape would need to run longer.

I suggest that you do your voice tape at a good recording studio with the professional help of a good engineer to assist you with the recording, editing, pacing and assembly of your tape. If you want the professional help of a voice tape producer, just ask around. I know that in Los Angeles there are several skilled and competent ones, and I'm sure that there are in New York as well as other larger cities.

You should book and plan to spend about an hour in the studio recording various things. Then, along with your producer or studio engineer, review, edit and tighten the material and assemble what will be a montage of what you've recorded. It is important to be prepared and organized before going into the recording studio, because you will be paying an hourly rate for the recording studio and engineer. It is possible to sometimes negotiate a flat fee with a studio to do your tape during "down times."

Once in a studio, if you find that you've recorded something that you like, but the piece is too long, there is nothing that says you must use this whole segment. Merely edit out sections of it and only put a portion of it on your tape.

Another thing you may choose to do is to embellish your tape with some production values by underscoring some of the voice tracks with library needle-drop music or perhaps include some sound effects in certain places.

Once you are satisfied with what you have assembled, then this becomes your voice-tape master. Initially, you should only make a limited number of audio cassettes or CDs from it. Don't make too many because you can always run off more copies later if you need more. When you revise your tape, which you will most certainly be doing, then you don't want to be stuck with too many copies of the last and outdated version.

You should now have something that does your voice fairly proud and, of course, something that you should now actively endeavor to get into the hands of a prospective commercial agent for their consideration. If an agent is interested in representing you, then the agent will likely suggest that you revise or modify your tape. This means incurring more costs because you will have to go back into the recording studio and restructure the master and run off some new copies of what you've just revised

Of course, if you are proficient at it, you could record, edit and assemble your voice tape right on your computer. To do this you would need a proper software program and a good microphone. Unless you are already set up for it, putting your voice tape together this way also means spending some money.

Once you are hired and do voices in actual commercials, you should try to get copies for possible inclusion on your voice tape. Include portions of this work, if you feel that it showcases other aspects of what you can do with your voice. Ultimately, the best examples on your tape will be examples of actual commercials, or portions thereof, that you have actually voiced. After the recording session is over, ask the producer or someone from the advertising agency who seems to be in charge, if it's ok for you to get a tape copy of the commercial. If it is, then always offer to pay for it, as recording studios don't run these copies off for free.

Your voice tape is always changing, so the only time that you would want to make lots of copies would be if you or your agent were planning to do an extensive mailing of the current version of your tape to prospective buyers of your voice.

Another expense to consider are the costs for the art design and printing of labels for your cassettes or CDs and any other materials such as stationary, mailing labels and business cards.

If you do plan to periodically send out mailing pieces promoting your tape, these too cost money, but remember that these impressions can be lasting ones. Put some good thought, design and creativity into what you send out. In terms of time and money, you could be looking at making a sizable investment. Of course, what you spend really depends upon what you can afford and what you feel an investment in your voice career is worth. This could be a few hundred to a few thousand dollars.

You should also consider becoming a dues-paying member in good standing in one or both of the unions that have jurisdiction over voice performances in commercials. These unions are American Federation of Television and Radio Artists (AFTRA) and the Screen Actors Guild (SAG). These unions have locals all over the country, so even if you're not doing your voice work in Los Angeles or New York, there's probably an AFTRA and SAG local in your area. For information about membership and qualification you can contact one or both of these union locals.

So now you have a voice tape; you also have an agent, and you belong to AFTRA, even SAG. So are we almost there yet? Not really.

In terms of what can seem like an endless pursuit of elusive voice bookings, it's right about here that some of the chaff begins to get separated from the wheat.

Much to their chagrin, beginning voice people soon find that most of the people they want to listen to their tape, as well as many who say they want to listen to their tape, really won't or don't.

In other words, when sending someone your voice tape unsolicited, the odds are very good that whoever you send it to will not listen to it. By the same token, when someone says, "Oh sure, send me your tape and I'll listen to it," the odds are only slightly better that they actually will. Even if they do listen to it, that doesn't necessarily mean that their socks will be blown off, nor is it any guarantee that there will be a resolve to cast you in their next commercial.

Speaking from my own experience, as a principal and the sole proprietor of a radio commercial production company, I found that hardly a day went by when I would not receive one or several voice tapes in the mail. Many tapes were also dropped off at my office. Hardly a day went by thereafter, when I would not receive follow-up phone calls from people all wanting to know if I had listened to their tape yet.

I confess. Most of these tapes fell upon deaf ears. I didn't have the time, patience or even the inclination to sit down on a regular daily basis and listen to all of them. Had I done so, I believe that in a short period of time I would have gone mad.

Perhaps you're thinking, "Well if that isn't a fine kettle of fish! So why do I even need a voice tape?" Trust me, you need one. If for no other reason, a voice tape confirms the fact that you are indeed a voice person, or at least that you're serious about being one. Think of it this way, most people have a voice, but how many have a tape?

"Wait a minute," you are possibly saying, "Are you saying that a voice tape is of no help in getting voice work?" Now you're jumping to conclusions and putting words in my mouth. That's not what I'm saying. Well, not exactly what I'm saying.

Voice tapes are like business cards. You may not hand them out to everybody you meet, and certainly not everybody that you do hand them out to will end up doing business with you. If or when some one asks, "Do you have a business card?" it's kind of important that you produce one and hand it to them.

If you have representation with a commercial talent agency, it is likely that a portion of your voice tape would be included in your agency's house tape.

The bottom line about a voice tape is that it's more likely to be seen than heard, which is not altogether a bad thing. Casting directors and agency producers are apt to know of a voice talent simply because they have come across their voice tape.

Even if they've merely seen the tape laying on someone's desk or it's laying on their desk, this is of value to the voice talent because it may pique someone's curiosity, especially when names are mentioned for audition consideration. This point also reinforces the importance of sending out occasional reminder mailing pieces.

All Things Considered, How Does One Get Work?

As best as I can tell, one gets voice work because someone who does the hiring is favorably familiar with that talent by having worked with them before. Familiarity with a voice talent usually has it's origins in listening to that talent's voice tape or knowing of the talent from their voice work in other commercials.

Last but not least, voice talent gets work because of an audition. Auditions are like the lottery. If you don't win one this time, you'll always have another chance to win another one. Of course, that's provided that you get called to audition for it.

The Recording Studio: The Commercial's Moment of Truth

Once the voice casting issue has been settled and the voices have been selected, the potential for brilliance or mediocrity is now about to begin. The next thing to decide is when to record and produce the radio commercial and then to select and schedule a studio and book the talent.

The decision when to record the commercial often depends on how soon the commercial has been scheduled to begin airing on the radio. If it's not for several weeks then there's usually no hurry. However, it's not unusual that the commercial be recorded as soon as possible because it is scheduled to start airing in a few days or even sooner.

A good recording studio, which is technically up to standard, is an essential prerequisite in the radio-commercial production process. Equally important is a skilled and proficient sound engineer, preferably one whom the director has a good rapport with and has worked with in the past.

To achieve the desired quality of the radio commercial, several fine tuned elements must be working during the recording session.

These elements, in order of importance are the radio commercial script itself and the voice talent.

Additionally, several other things impact the commercial's potential. Prominent among these is that the one directing the commercial be skilled and experienced. Radio commercials do not produce themselves, and inexperienced directors who fumble their way through a recording session don't do much better. Voice talent always look to someone who is in control of the session, and they are most responsive to a director who knows what they're doing.

The next thing of importance has to do with the karma of the recording session. If there are good and relaxed vibrations in the control room, then the stage is set for a pleasant environment where the voice players can comfortably perform and excel in the studio.

When humor is in the making, a pleasant environment is especially important. For the commercial to be fun, so too should be the atmosphere of the recording session. If those in the control room are uptight, tentative and stressed, that can only serve to dampen the spontaneity and spirit of the talents' performances.

So who should or shouldn't be at the recording session? That depends largely upon the size of the control room and how many people can be comfortably accommodated. Often, there will be people from the advertising agency and the client advertiser who are there at the session merely to watch. Even though their presence is not required or needed, I personally have never had a problem with them being there, as long as they don't suddenly leap up and start assisting in the production of the commercial.

Here is my short list of the people who I feel should definitely be present at the recording session, in addition, of course, to the sound engineer and the voice talent.

1. The Producer/Director. This person should be in command and control of the session and should be the only one who directs the talent. Any other input for the talent should be funneled to the director and not directly to the talent. Talent should never be put in a situation where they are compelled to alter their performance by responding to conflicting direction from more than one director.

2. The writer of the commercial. Sometimes this person will be the one directing the commercial. Even if they are not directing the commercial, the writer's presence is important. Often the director will work closely with the writer during the session. In the event that copy revisions are needed for time purposes, then the writer should be responsible for making those changes.

3. The agency broadcast producer. Occasionally this person will be the one directing the commercial. However, the agency producer's responsibilities are usually administrative and logistical, having to do with studio and talent scheduling, as well as paperwork and contracts for AFTRA union talent reports.

4. An agency account executive and/or someone representing the client advertiser, who has the

ultimate authority to approve what is taking place during the recording session.

I have, on occasion, produced and directed commercials with as many as five or six agency people in attendance. At a point well into the recording session I discover that none of them, not the creative director, account executive or even a partner or the owner of the agency, has any authority to approve what is being recorded and produced.

It is most disconcerting, even somewhat maddening, that at a critical point in the session we are obliged to ask the talent to "stand by" as everything comes to a halt. This delay is to make a long distance call so that "the client" can listen to our selected "takes" and either approve or disapprove what's been recorded thus far.

Predictably, the client will often find fault and then proceed to attempt to fix something that assuredly is not broken. Taking command of the session via long distance, the client often proceeds to redo all that has been done up to this point. Invariably what the client "re-does" is re-direct the voice talent to energize their delivery and emphasize certain words, like the name of the product. This is precisely the moment when what has, up to this point, been a fine recording session, suddenly turns into a fine fiasco.

The analogy of the patient undergoing surgery is apt once more. How irregular would it be if a surgeon was obliged to stop in the middle of a simple operation so that the patient's cousin could come in and approve of how the surgery was going? And what if the cousin thought he could make some improvements on it? Does the cousin throw on a little blue gown, scrub up and push the surgeon aside and proceed to perform the rest of the operation himself? What about the patient? Does he pull through or does he just croak right there on the operating table?

If it's imperative that someone at the client level approve and sign off on the recording session, then that someone should be present at the session. If that person is too busy or important to be at the session, then they should relegate the responsibility to somebody else who can be at the session.

Unfortunately, today there is a growing shortage of client advertisers who actually trust and empower their advertising agency to make simple commercial production decisions, like selecting a specific "take" for a radio commercial that's being recorded. Decisions like this are fundamental to the process of making advertising.

This leads one to wonder: Isn't this what advertisers hire advertising agencies to do in the first place? You know, make advertising?

The Phantom Recording Session: Where Is Everybody?

It's called a "phone patch" and it's a very common way of producing radio commercials these days. It's not the best way, mind you, but it is an expedient way nonetheless. It's all done over the phone.

Basically a phone-patch recording session works like this: Let's say the advertising agency producing the commercial is in Detroit and the voice talent they are using is in Los Angeles. Two recording studios will be booked at the same time. A studio in Detroit, where the agency will "direct" from, and a studio in Los Angeles, where the talent will "voice" from. These studios will be connected with special digital phone lines or via a satellite.

Once set up, the agency director can talk directly to the talent through earphone headsets. What is then subsequently recorded in the studio in Los Angeles will simultaneously be transmitted, received and recorded at the studio in Detroit.

A phone-patch recording session is a reasonably viable and expedient way to record a one-voice read, such as a monologue or an announcer's lines for either a radio or TV commercial voice-over. Phone-patch sessions do get a little tricky though when an agency producer attempts to direct several voices, as well as work with the engineer in the selection and placement of sound effects and/or music tracks.

From a voice talent's perspective, it's a little like performing in a vacuum. You're performing for people who are there, but they're only there on the phone.

The Last Act: Finishing the Radio Commercial

W hen a voice talent shows up at the appointed time for a recording session, with rare exception, they are genuinely pleased to have been chosen to work in the commercial. Professional voice people like nothing more than to be booked for a voice job. Of course, they like the idea that they are getting paid for it, but it's really the working part that actors love.

Once behind the microphone, it's a voice actor's fervent desire to perform to the complete satisfaction and delight of all who are in the control room.

If a voice talent is someone that the director has never worked with before, it's always a good idea for the director to spend a few moments getting acquainted with the talent before going into the studio and proceeding to work. It is also important to be cognizant of the fact that the voice talent, in all likelihood, has worked under similar commercial recording session situations many times before. Therefore, the director should never presume that they are clueless babes in the advertising woods.

A radio commercial production session should be looked upon as a place where a creative collaboration takes place. This collaboration doesn't just involve the writer and the director, but it also includes the recording engineer and the voice talent. The director is the one in charge, but these others should be allowed to feel that any creative input they might have is welcome.

When producing and directing a radio commercial, here are some of my personal *do's* and *don'ts*:

When you are booking a recording studio, do make sure that you book and schedule enough time to properly record, assemble and mix the commercial you are producing. Conversely, be careful about overbooking more studio time than you will actually need. Even though you finish early, many studios will still charge for the entire block of time that was originally booked.

One hour should be sufficient to record the voice tracks for one commercial. Depending upon how complex the production elements are—sound effects or music cues—the assembly and mixing of all the elements can take anywhere from one to three hours for each commercial.

Of course, if the producer is obliged to stop the session in progress in order to play voice takes over the phone for the client and make client suggested changes, then more studio time needs to be factored in.

I would say that typically an average fully produced radio commercial, from start to finish, should take about two to three hours to record, assemble and mix. To be on the safe side, it's always better to overbook than underbook. That's because very often another session may have already been scheduled to begin right after your session has been scheduled to end.

In the event that you're not finished, you must relinquish the studio and then scramble around and try to book more studio time to finish later. That's a huge *don't*, especially when copies of the commercial are supposed to be quickly dispatched to the radio stations to meet an imminent airing schedule.

Once you have estimated how much time you will need and you have booked the studio, you're ready to start the show.

The first and foremost *don't* is don't start directing the talent right off the bat. Do give the talent a chance to rehearse and familiarize themselves with the script in the first couple of takes. It is even a good idea to tell the engineer to roll tape and record these initial read-throughs. You never know when something wonderful might happen, even during these rehearsals.

Time these takes to get an idea of how long the commercial is actually running. Is it right on time, or is it too short or too long? If it's running ten or more seconds longer than the allotted sixty seconds of time, then this is when someone, like the writer, should start figuring out how and where to take time out of the script.

During these initial takes, don't be too concerned with how the talent is reading the lines. Don't try to establish the actor's character at this point. Often a director will have a predilection of how they want the lines delivered. Don't impart that "direction" until the talent has been allowed to deliver the lines as they intuitively feel that the lines should be delivered. Very often, the talent's own innate way of interpreting and delivering the lines is much better than the writer's or director's sense of how the line should be read.

Once you are ready to start "directing" the commercial, don't ask your talent to become a "voice pirate" by asking them to do or try to do someone else. If that someone else that the director is asking the talent to "do" is alive, working and available, then by all means that is the person who should have been booked for this voice job.

Hiring a specific voice talent because of their skill at impersonating a well-known person is a different matter. In this case, there are legalities to consider, particularly if the famous person being impersonated is alive. Even if the person is deceased, it may still be necessary to obtain clearances and permission from that person's estate. At the very least, the commercial should incorporate or conclude with a disclaimer to the effect "Celebrity voice impersonated."

Quite often, directors will give the talent a "line reading." In this case, the actor is essentially being asked to mimic the director's read, even going so far as to parrot the same inflections and vocal rhythms. Some voice talents are more adroit at mimicking than others.

Sometimes a director will give a voice talent a line reading for no other reason than that is merely how the director would deliver the line. The director is not the one who's in the commercial delivering the line, so that sort of direction is very high on my list of directorial *don'ts.*

A director's line reading is only called for when it's necessary to clarify the meaning of the line or if the actor is mispronouncing or incorrectly interpreting it and therefore not giving the read the intended meaning.

Pursuant to this, don't ask the talent to go up or down on a certain word. Which ever way the actor goes on the word, whether it's up, down or sideways, the important thing is that the delivery of the word should sound natural and comfortable.

Don't over-direct. Voice actors by and large have a very good idea what they're doing and how to do it. A good director is one who recognizes if and when something is right, even though that may not necessarily be what they were initially looking for in their direction.

Here's some of my favorite cliché and over-worked pieces of direction. Do try to avoid them if you can.

"Let's try it again, and this time have fun with it." "Okay, forget what I just told you and go back to what you were doing before." "That was perfect! Let's just do a few more for protection." "I think we've got it. That looks like a wrap, but now is there anything else *you'd* like to try?"

It doesn't seem to happen that often, but sometimes the best read actually happens in the very first take. Bingo. The chemistry, timing, pacing, delivery, spontaneity, everything is all there in the first read. "Thank you very much, everybody can go home."

Surprisingly, it probably happens a lot more often than is realized. "Take number one? Impossible." Believe me. It's possible.

Don't overtake. Call it insecurity, procrastination or just a futile search for the Holy Grail of reads, there are certain directors, whom I call "take junkies," who are obsessive about doing takes. When turned loose in a recording studio control room, this type of director will press on and on with take after take. This director fails to recognize that probably the best read of the commercial happened twenty or thirty takes before. As a matter of fact, any number of previous takes could be fine, but this director wouldn't recognize it.

Doing a myriad of takes with the idea that you will then cut and paste together something magical with a word or two here and a line or two there is an exercise in futility. Don't spend unnecessary and costly studio time going through that drill.

Contrary to unconventional wisdom, over-killing in the "takes" department doesn't necessarily resuscitate or breathe any new life into a commercial. So, do know when enough is enough.

Here is a short list of what to listen for in a given take:

Is the take on time, or is too long? If it's a great take, can these extra seconds be edited out? If not, would another take with a faster read make the commercial sound too rushed? Was it a great take except that a word or a line was flubbed? Can that word or line be recorded again as a "wild" read and be edited into the take?

Seldom do I ever go back and review each and every take. If I do, it's only to look for a better or clearer read on a specific word or phrase to pull and then cut into our selected take.

When evaluating a take, do it on the basis of its overall feel. Don't just focus on specific words or lines. Poorly read or flubbed words or lines can be lifted from a previous take. If a better read in previous takes doesn't exist, it can be corrected simply by re-recording it as a wild line.

The announcer copy, which the client advertiser has invariably deemed to be the most important aspect of the commercial, should always be the first thing that's recorded. The reason for this is because if it becomes necessary to tamper with the commercial and cut copy, the announcer words are the ones usually most sheltered from any tampering. What the announcer has to say, no matter how mundane or trite, is pretty much etched in stone.

I suggest getting a good comfortable read and also a quicker usable read that can be used if need be. If there are two good announcer reads, one taking 20 seconds to deliver and another taking 18 seconds, then you know that the dialogue or ensemble players have 40 to 42 seconds for their lines. However, if there are about 3 seconds of sound effects to be included, then the players would only have 37 to 39 seconds for their lines.

Once the announcer's lines have been satisfactorily recorded, it's a good idea to have them stick around for a few minutes so the director can have the dialogue or ensemble players run through and time their lines. When assured that any potential changes or copy cuts will not involve the announcer's lines, the announcer can be released. Now the other voices can be recorded to their appropriate times. Once a selected take is made and any subsequent wild lines have been recorded, the voice talent can be dismissed.

The commercial is then ready to be assembled with the necessary elements of sound effects, background ambiance and music. These elements are positioned and placed against the voice tracks and then mixed together. All of these tracks are then balanced to the satisfaction of the producer and then transferred to a DAT master. Now, the radio commercial is actually finished. From here, copies of the commercial are sent to the radio stations that will be airing the commercial.

Whether listeners will respond to the radio commercial essentially depends on six variables.

1. Is the product that's being advertised something that a significant number of listeners will need or want to buy?

2. What the advertiser says about the product in the commercial.

3. How the advertiser says it in the commercial.

4. The duration and frequency of the commercial's radio air-play.

5. The availability of the product where it's intended to be sold.

6. Finally, is the product as good as the commercial suggests that it is? Each of these variables will significantly impact the success or failure of the radio commercial.

Chapter 20

Thanks for Listening

The medium of radio has come a long way and gone through many dynamic and exciting transformations since 1920 when the Harding/Cox presidential returns were first aired. Radio commercials, however, have just been along for the ride.

What I have attempted to point out in this book is that if advertisers are to realize the potential rewards of radio, then they and their advertising agencies must make the commitment to use this medium much more creatively. By recognizing that people listen to the radio but only hear the commercials, then hopefully radio advertising might start speaking up. Some of the techniques and procedures I have detailed, along with my forty-something years of fun, fame and frustration in the business of making entertaining radio commercials, will, I trust, be a source of enlightenment as well as encouragement

I have, therefore, changed my mind about Fred Petzel, the hog calling guy. I am sure that he was a wonderful person and extremely skilled at what he did. However, I don't think that he qualifies anymore to be on my radio advertising pundits' list. That's because if anybody is really going to get those piggies to perk up their ears and come running for what's in the trough, then the "voice" better give them more than just the same old sooey-sooey.

Bibliography

Anobile, Richard J., ed. 1974. *Who's on First?* Flare Books published by Avon.

Nachman, Gerald. 1998. *Raised on Radio.* New York: Pantheon Books.

Schulberg, Bob. 1989. *Radio Advertising: The Authoritative Handbook.* Illinois: NTC Business Books.

Order Form

To order any of the books listed below, you can write to us directly, contact your local book store, FAX, or order online at: www.GabrielBooks.com

Hearing Voices: Creating, Voicing and Producing Great Radio Commercials, by Alan Barzman $19.95
A rare insiders view of the world of radio commercial production.

Roller Hockey: The Game Within the Game, by Warren Taylor $19.95
An in-depth guide to this growing sport. Ideal for coaches, players and fans.

Books for Financial and Business Growth:

Couples and Money, by Victoria Collins, PhD $13.95
A vital guide for couples to thrive financially and emotionally. It provides exercises and instructions for couples to talk about money. Recommended by Consumer Credit Counseling Service.

Wealth On Any Income, by Rennie Gabriel,
CLU, CFP (UCLA Instructor) $17.95
Move from creating financial goals to achieving them. Covers both the emotional and practical aspects of handling money effectively. Endorsed by Mark Victor Hansen, co-author of the *Chicken Soup for the Soul*® series.

Wealth On Any Income cassette tape program $59.00
Five hours read by Rennie Gabriel from his book. It is a comprehensive, but simple to use, program for anyone to handle money effectively, get out of debt, live within their income, start investing with as little as $100 and ultimately create financial independence. Includes the full book and two spending registers.

How to Outwit and Outsell Your Competition, by Shirley Lee $14.95
Grow your business 50-200% per year using little known, powerful strategies that cannot fail. Avoid costly marketing blunders by learning the common mistakes.

The REALTOR® Series:

Our REALTOR® series of books will show you how to get the best deal when buying a home. They are currently available for the states listed below and are all $17.95 each.

For additional information, please call (800) 940-2622.

How to Make Your REALTOR® Get You the Best Deal,

    Colorado 2ⁿᵈ Edition
    Idaho Edition
    Indiana Edition
    Illinois Edition

Kansas Edition
Louisiana Edition
Michigan Edition
Minnesota Edition
Montana Edition
Nevada Edition
New York Edition
Oklahoma Edition
Southern California Edition
Texas Edition
Washington Edition

Order Form—Please Copy, Fill Out, Mail, Fax, Phone or Go Online

Name_____

Address_____

City, State, zip_____

Daytime phone (____)_____

e-mail address_____

Product Description	Quantity	Total
_____	_____	$_____
_____	_____	$_____
_____	_____	$_____
_____	_____	$_____

Sales tax, (only for orders delivered in CA) 8% $_____

Shipping and handling, $4 per book or tape $_____

Total: $_____

❑ check enclosed $_____

❑ please charge my M/C or Visa #_____

Expiration date_____

Signature as on the card_____

Mail to: Gabriel Publications
14340 Addison Street #101
Sherman Oaks, CA 91423-1832
or fax to (818) 990-8631
www.GabrielBooks.com